T0303741

WALKING IN
ITALY'S CINQUE TERRE

WALKING IN ITALY'S CINQUE TERRE

MONTEROSSO AL MARE, VERNAZZA, CORNIGLIA, MANAROLA AND RIOMAGGIORE

by Gillian Price

JUNIPER HOUSE, MURLEY MOSS,
OXENHOLME ROAD, KENDAL, CUMBRIA LA9 7RL
www.cicerone.co.uk

© Gillian Price 2019
First edition 2019
Reprinted 2023 (with updates)
ISBN: 978 1 85284 973 3

Printed in China on responsibly sourced paper on behalf of Latitude Press Ltd.
A catalogue record for this book is available from the British Library.
All photographs are by the author unless otherwise stated.

Route mapping by Lovell Johns www.lovelljohns.com
Contains OpenStreetMap.org data © OpenStreetMap
contributors, CC-BY-SA. NASA relief data courtesy of ESRI

Dedication

As well as my special companion Nicola, I was very fortunate to enjoy the company of dear Alison in the Cinque Terre. Her enthusiasm never flagged even when faced with endless flights of steep steps that always seemed to go uphill. (Could it have been the promise of gelato?)

Updates to this Guide

While every effort is made by our authors to ensure the accuracy of guidebooks as they go to print, changes can occur during the lifetime of an edition. Any updates that we know of for this guide will be on the Cicerone website (www. cicerone.co.uk/973/updates), so please check before planning your trip. We also advise that you check information about such things as transport, accommodation and shops locally. Even rights of way can be altered over time.

The route maps in this guide are derived from publicly available data, databases and crowd-sourced data. As such they have not been through the detailed checking procedures that would generally be applied to a published map from an official mapping agency, although naturally we have reviewed them closely in the light of local knowledge as part of the preparation of this guide.

We are always grateful for information about any discrepancies between a guidebook and the facts on the ground, sent by email to updates@cicerone. co.uk or by post to Cicerone, Juniper House, Murley Moss, Oxenholme Road, Kendal, LA9 7RL.

Register your book: To sign up to receive free updates, special offers and GPX files where available, register your book at www.cicerone.co.uk.

Front cover: A marvellous panoramic point overlooking the southern side of Vernazza (Walk 5)

CONTENTS

Riomaggiore is a long way below (Walk 11)

Symbols used on route maps

route
alternative route
start point
finish point
start/finish point
route direction
woodland
urban areas
station/railway
peak
building
church/monastery/cross
castle or tower
pass
bus stop
ferry
ferry route
tourist info
car park
other feature

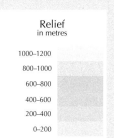

Relief
in metres

1000–1200
800–1000
600–800
400–600
200–400
0–200

SCALE: 1:50,000

Contour lines are drawn at 25m intervals and highlighted at 100m intervals.

GPX files for all routes can be downloaded free at www.cicerone.co.uk/973/GPX.

Colourful fishing boats in Vernazza harbour

Manarola has a magnificent setting

INTRODUCTION

The seafront of Riomaggiore is a celebrated spot around sunset

Pastel coloured villages are wedged into dizzy rock promontories over the sparkling sea, defying gravity. Between them, row upon row of man-made terraces appear to cascade down vertiginous mountainsides. Neck-craningly steep paths lead to spectacular lookouts that take your breath away. Secluded coves with turquoise water are the reward for venturing down hundreds of knee-challenging stone steps. Brilliant carpets of Mediterranean wildflowers add to the irresistible charm, as does the superb cuisine based on locally grown olives and wine. This is Liguria in north west Italy, and these are the Cinque Terre.

We're talking about a mere 12km of rugged coast that is home to gliding seagulls and the 'Famous Five'. There's nowhere else like it, and it is duly recognised with UNESCO World Heritage Site status.

So what exactly are the Cinque Terre? And why do people flock here from all over the globe? The 'five lands' as they translate literally, correspond to the villages of Monterosso, Vernazza, Corniglia, Manarola and Riomaggiore. Nowadays the Cinque Terre are home to around 4400 residents in all, many of whom work in tourism. Starting in the late Middle Ages they were built up bit by bit

11

around narrow steep *arpaie* stairways and *carrugi* alleys suitable for donkeys and people. Every available scrap of land was exploited for the tower-like houses constructed one atop the other. Their coastal location set them up as vulnerable targets for raids by Saracen pirates who plagued the Ligurian coast for centuries and led to the construction of the many landmark watchtowers. As of the 1200s these were further fortified when the villages passed under the control of the mighty maritime republic of Genoa.

Land-based products such as wine, olives, oil, capers, citrus fruits and chestnut flour were once carried by man and mule downhill for shipping to market ports such as Genoa. The coast and villages are still linked one to the other – and the terraced fields – by ancient pathways, mostly with heart-stopping flights of stone steps. Due to the geography – hundreds of metres below a towering cliff ridge spelled isolation for centuries – the paths were the main way for the inhabitants to get around. (These days a handful of roads reach the seafront settlements, while a landmark railway burrows through the mountainsides.) So what better way to explore this unique area than on foot? *Sentiero* is the Italian for 'path', and there's certainly no lack of them here, all well marked and signposted. These are simply superb routes for walkers, who flock here to discover a paradise.

EXPLORING THE CINQUE TERRE

In addition to the five principal villages and hinterland which come under the protection of the Parco Nazionale Cinque Terre (www.parconazionale5terre.it) this guidebook includes neighbouring settlements that offer worthwhile pathways. These are seafront Levanto in the north, mountainside Campiglia further down, then charming Porto Venere at the southern extremity on the opening of the Gulf of La Spezia. Each place has a distinct character and for different reasons makes a great base for a walking holiday. All are easily accessible by public transport, and have tourist and park info offices, ATM cash points, as well as grocery shops, cafés and restaurants, and masses of accommodation. The sole exception is Campiglia which has no info office or ATM. Helpful maps of the villages can be found in Appendix A.

Starting in the north west, **Levanto** is a natural entry gate to the Cinque Terre for visitors arriving by rail from the Ligurian regional capital of Genoa. The no-frills town has plenty of advantages, ranging from easy access, lower prices and a decent beach, though it is rather lacking in charm. Walk 1 starts its marvellous traverse here.

Separated from Levanto and the rest of the world by a high ridge culminating in the rugged headland of Punta Mesco, spread-out **Monterosso al Mare** (with a population of 1468) is the only one of the Cinque Terre to boast a beach worthy of that name

THE TERRACED LANDSCAPE

With the exception of Monterosso, the Cinque Terre were traditionally agricultural rather than being oriented towards fishing. Over the centuries some 2000 hectares (65% of the total land) of the outrageously steep hillsides from the water's edge up to 400m above sea level have been crafted into immaculate terracing with *cian* or strips of arable land, by generation upon generation of hard-working farmers. The land first needed to be deforested, roots and rocks removed, then levelled out as far as possible. Soil was carried in, and using the stones removed earlier, painstakingly buttressed with the construction of a mind-boggling estimated 7000km of dry stone walls. Run-off channels were excavated alongside. The terracing requires regular expert maintenance to counter landslips and wall bulges that can lead to collapses and threaten paths. Crops such as olives are still grown as well as grapes. The traditional system for planting vines was referred to as the *vigna bassa* low vine, though arbours and rows have now replaced this. It has been calculated that each hectare of vineyard is supported by 4000m² of stone.

September is usually the time for the grape harvest, and the fruit is transported to a roadhead on ingenious monorails.

Terraced hillsides overlooking Corniglia

Magnificent Vernazza seen from a cliffside path

– an inviting expanse of golden sand stretching along an ample bay. As well as a fair amount of level land, Monterosso has roads and a modern section called Fegina with a batch of hotels, not to mention a railway station. A pleasant seafront promenade runs through a road tunnel to the old *centro storico*, passing a watchtower occupying a rocky point. The great Italian poet Eugenio Montale, winner of the Nobel Prize for Literature in 1975, spent his childhood years on vacation here and the landscape is a constant in his work. Walks 2, 3 and 4 explore the wooded hills and coastal track starting here.

Next along is superbly photogenic **Vernazza** snuggling in a secluded cove. A modest pocket of sand and harbour protected by breakwaters is overlooked by the elegant Romanesque church of Santa Margherita d'Antiochia. Uphill is a remnant of the Castello Doria, a Genoese construction with a medieval watchtower later converted into a windmill, not to mention its use as an anti-aircraft structure during the Second World War. The village name derives from Vulnetia, an ancient Roman family, though the first historical records date back to the 1000s. Once an independent village (that carried out its own raids!), it was brought under Genoa in 1211 and became a strategic base against arch rival Pisa. A delightful place to stay, Vernazza has 852 permanent inhabitants, a railway station carved into the hillside, and is the start for Walk 5.

The middle village of the five, charming **Corniglia** is by far the quietest thanks to its elevated position perched on a vertiginous clifftop headland. This may explain the origin of its name from 'corno' rocky spur. From the railway station you go up the famous Scalinata Lardarina, a zigzagging brick stairway composed of 382 steps and 33 ramps – though there's also a bus run via the road. In addition to elegant churches and cosy houses, it boasts a belvedere terrace for legendary sunsets over the Ligurian Sea. The 195 resident numbers are boosted by those who move back in the warmer months, as happens in the other *terre*. Challenging Walks 6 and 7 begin at Corniglia.

The following stop is beautiful **Manarola**. Here a divine sheltered bay and harbour are popular with swimmers who clamber up rock pinnacles to dive into the clear blue sea. The houses here are squeezed into a narrow valley, leaving plenty of space for the extensive terraced vineyards above. The name may derive from *magna rota*, the large wheel of the water-driven mill that can still be seen in the main street – a convincing explanation as a river crossed by 11 stone bridges flowed here until the 1950–1970s when it was paved over. Another mammoth task was the long pedestrian tunnel that burrows under a cliff connecting the railway station. Walks 8 and 9 commence here. Manarola has 353 residents, counting the upper

hamlets such as lovely Volastra, visited on Walk 7.

The last of the Cinque Terre is lively **Riomaggiore**. According to local hearsay it was founded by eighth century Greeks fleeing persecution in their homeland. The name derives from the Rivus Major watercourse, now hidden away beneath tarmac. Over time Riomaggiore grew into a sizeable village, typical narrow alleys lined with tower-like buildings piled on top of each other and looked over by a humble castle; the last census gave a population of 1542. The seafront is an especially celebrated spot of an evening when the orange rays of the setting sun light up the coloured houses that appear to topple off the cliffs. Over winter the traditional fishing boats are dragged out of the water and 'parked' in piles to keep them safe during storms. Circuit Walks 10 and 11 begin here, as does the extended traverse Walk 12.

Perched at 400m altitude on a panoramic saddle boasting marvellous views looking both to the Gulf of La Spezia and over the Ligurian Sea, laidback **Campiglia** sees few visitors. With a permanent population of 60 that swells during the summer months, the mountainside hamlet is an inviting spot and is the start for Walks 13 and 14 that visit secluded coves. It has a good bus service to La Spezia and also offers groceries, a handful of restaurants and accommodation.

Another 'ring-in' in the south east is utterly charming **Porto Venere** that occupies a low rocky promontory at the opening of the gulf. The heart of Porto Venere is 'La Palazzata', an unusually tall photogenic block of old fortified houses along the rocky seafront, a watercolour artist's dream. The name Porto Venere (port of Venus) is derived from a long-gone temple to the Greco-Roman goddess of love who rose majestically from the foaming waves that break onto the headland. The iconic church of San Pietro now stands on the spot. High above on Monte Muzzerone is landmark Castello Doria, a serious deterrent to anyone once considering an attack on the Genoese town. Porto Venere was a location for the marvellous 1975 film *The Count of Monte-Cristo* though an earlier claim to fame came from the English poet Byron who enjoyed swimming across to Lerici to visit his friends Shelley et al; the Gulf of La Spezia is also known as the Gulf of the Poets. Porto Venere is easily reached by bus or ferry from La Spezia, and Walk 15 starts there.

Directly opposite is the car-less island of Palmaria, explored in Walk 16 thanks to a boat service. As well as paths, beaches and abandoned forts and quarries, it has renowned restaurants and even a guesthouse. Together with the minor islands Tino and Tinetto, Palmaria, Porto Venere and its mountainous hinterland come under the protective wing of the Parco Naturale Porto Venere (www.parconaturaleportovenere.it).

The colourful Palazzata at Porto Venere

LANDMARK YEARS 1874 AND 2011

The year 1874 was a landmark one for the Cinque Terre as it was then that the railway was opened. It changed life for ever for the tiny cliffside villages. A remarkable feat of engineering, it burrows through the sheer mountainsides high over the sea between the naval city of La Spezia on its gulf and the Ligurian seaside of Sestri Levante. Travelling on it is a bit like an amusemet park ride. You depart from a modern city, the train goes into a dark tunnel and abracadabra, in a matter of minutes you're transported into the wonder world of the Cinque Terre. The railway stations themselves are amazing, squeezed under houses, half the platform in a tunnel in many cases, or at the foot of awesome cliffs only metres away from breaking waves.

For a completely different reason, another landmark year was 2011. On October 25 a freak cloudburst over Liguria washed down tons of soil and rock through Monterosso and Vernazza. Flooding was widespread and several lives were lost. The villages were devastated, their main streets transformed into a dangerous watercourse and two metres of mud and soil left behind, reaching the first floor of buildings. The only reminders nowadays are the startling photos near Vernazza railway station.

WALKING

The footpaths in the Cinque Terre are open to everyone. It can get crowded, but quite frankly it's inspiring to see so many people out there on foot. However despite the vicinity of the sea, these routes are not a matter of a simple beachfront promenade. The terrain is rocky and often near-vertical, and flights of steps with ongoing ups and downs are the flavour of the day. Holidaymakers in the Cinque Terre need to be reasonably fit. But don't be put off, there's plenty for both novices as well as experienced walkers used to strenuous climbs. Choose your route carefully, enjoy yourself and keep safe. There are always guided walks – an excellent way to explore the paths in the company of local experts.

The famous SVA – Sentiero Verde Azzurro – also known as n.2, is a multi-stage coastal path that links the villages. This is the only path subject to an entry fee, payable at the checkpoints near the path start (the national park allocates the money to path maintenance). Note: At the time of writing, only three stretches were open: Monterosso to Vernazza then Vernazza to Corniglia, as well as a very short section from Riomaggiore towards Manarola. The remaining sections are undergoing reconstruction and maintenance – an ongoing situation. Either pay single entry or buy a Cinque Terre Card. Other paths are free of charge.

A flight of steps climbing alongside an old stone wall and gardens (Walk 4)

Creating a short trek

In addition to the 16 single-day walks described in this guidebook, an exciting 3-4 day trek traverse can be made from Levanto all the way across to Porto Venere with a stop in a different memorable village each night. Simply string together Walks 1, 4, 5, 7, 9 and 12.

A marvellous array of Mediterranean plants flourish in the Cinque Terre. Close to the sea, rock cracks and shingle are the habitat of attractive rock samphire (*Crithmum maritimum*), called sea fennel (*finocchio marino*) in Italian. It has light green fleshy leaves and modest light yellow flowers that produce distinctive tangy seeds which are used in cooking. Another important plant for the kitchen is the caper, a straggling vine with pretty white-pink flowers that flourishes on sun-scorched stone walls. Its buds, gathered for preserving with salt or vinegar, were once an important crop here.

The dry rocky terrain is the perfect habitat for hardy maquis herbs. Rosemary, lavender, mint, oregano and thyme fill the air with their delicious scents through spring and summer. Especially fragrant is everlasting (*Helichrysum stoechas*) which sports tiny woolly yellow blooms and slim long silvery leaves that exude a curry-like aroma when crushed.

Bushy dwarf fan palms (*Chamaerops humilis*) are dotted along the coast. Europe's sole native palm, this relic of the tropical Cretaceous period 80 million years ago was once used widely for baskets and brooms. It has tiny yellow bell-shaped blooms which give way to orange berries. Broom comes in many shapes and sizes. With clusters of bright yellow flowers into the summer months, an outstanding example is thorny broom (*Calicotome spinosa*) which forms dense impenetrable thickets, protection against soil erosion.

Higher up, the steep slopes of the Cinque Terre overlooking the sea are thick with woody shrubs. Curious tree spurge (*Euphorbia dendroides*) is widespread. It grows in low bushes that form a dome and produces blooms that are remarkably similar to Shrek's ears, no less. The tiny bell-like blooms of tree heather (*Erica arborea*) turn hillsides into a sea of white at the end of winter, while as spring gets under way rock roses (*Cistus*) add splashes of pastel with their pink, yellow and purple flowers as thin as tissue paper. Myrtle shrubs (*Myrtus communis*) have small shiny green leaves, pretty delicate white blossom and dark berries widely used to flavour liquors.

Woodland is dominated by Mediterranean evergreens such as holm oak (*Quercus ilex*) that bears acorns, once fed to livestock. The curious strawberry tree (*Arbutus unedo*) is more colourful; it is hung with delicate white bell-shaped flowers at the

Anti-clockwise from top left: *Tree heather explodes with masses of tiny white bells at the end of winter; Attractive thorny broom forms impenetrable thickets; Delicate rock rose flowers*

same time as red-orange fruit, edible but lumpy.

Chestnut trees form dense thickets, their bright green palmed leaves fading to crunchy russet as the months pass. Long abandoned by man, they continue to provide nutty fruit in prickly casings like hedgehogs, thudding to the ground in an autumn breeze. As the steep terrain here is unsuitable for growing wheat, chestnuts were once a key foodstuff, gathered and ground into flour, and even exported.

Birdwatchers won't be disappointed in the Cinque Terre. The elegant peregrine falcon (*Falco peregrinus*) treats walkers to exciting aerial displays as it zooms over the coast hunting smaller birds. Huge numbers of raucous and gregarious seagulls breed successfully along the rugged coastline, building nests on impossible cliffs. The magnificent herring gull (*Larus argentatus*) prefers the island of Palmaria, which is also home to cormorants that fish off the rocks. The northern gannet (*Morus bassanus)* has recently begun nesting very close to the waterfront at Porto Venere.

Multi-coloured lizards scuttling over rocks are the most common land-based wildlife in this part of Liguria. Otherwise commonly spotted on stone walls where it hunts for dinner, is the attractive green whip snake (*Hierophis viridiflavus*) which actually looks black, with lots of yellow chequered patches and stripes. While not venomous, it has been known to bite people. On the other hand vipers, recognisable by their silvery-grey diamond markings, are both poisonous and thankfully rare. Should you encounter one sunbaking on a path, give it time to slither away – it's probably more frightened than you in any case.

Four-legged animals include timid foxes. There are also wild boar which tramp the hills in search of edible roots and nuts, leaving a muddy trail of devastation as they upturn stones as they dig. Despite their bulk and size, they are notoriously shy so walkers need not worry about an encounter.

Dolphins as well as whales cruise off the coast at different times of year, and an offshore Marina Reserve restricts human activity.

GETTING THERE AND GETTING AROUND

Getting to the Cinque Terre couldn't be easier – catch the train. If you're arriving from the south and Tuscany (via Pisa with its international airport www.pisa-airport.com) then the animated naval port city of La Spezia will be your gateway. Whereas from the north you'll pass through the regional capital of Genoa (whose airport is www.airport.genova.it) before reaching the key railway station of Levanto. Fast through trains between Genoa and Pisa don't stop at all the Cinque Terre stations so on the stretch between Levanto and La Spezia it's best to catch the local all-stops service. Known as the Cinque Terre Express, it runs every half hour from spring to autumn and approximately hourly the rest of the year. All train timetables can be found at www.trenitalia.com.

To move from one of the Cinque Terre villages to another, a good ferry service plies the coast from spring to autumn – details at www.navigazionegolfodeipoeti.it. Lastly, a handy Explora bus also runs between La Spezia and some of the villages – see www.explora5terre.it.

There are roads to each of the villages but they are narrow, steep, traffic restricted and essential for

Vernazza's railway station is squeezed in between houses

residents and deliveries. The few car parks are understandably expensive. Bottom line: visitors should not plan on arriving by car.

Porto Venere is not on the railway line so to reach it either catch a ferry (see above) or ATC bus (www. atcesercizio.it) from La Spezia.

INFORMATION

The Parco Nazionale delle Cinque Terre (www.parconazionale5terre. it) has information points with helpful multilingual staff at all the railway stations, including La Spezia. Guided walks are organised and maps are on sale as well as park cards. The Cinque Terre Card covers fee-paying paths, WCs, local buses and guided walks (a great way to visit the area with a local

A single day Cinque Terre card

expert). Another version – the Cinque Terre Treno MS Card – also includes local train travel. Most villages also have a tourist office, often known as a Pro Loco. See Appendix C for the complete lists with websites and contact details.

WHEN TO GO

Any time of year is feasible to visit the beautiful Cinque Terre and each season has its special charm with different light conditions and vegetation colours. Spring (April to June) and autumn (September and October) are considered the best times to go and mean avoiding the heat of the summer months. So those are understandably the busiest times. Winter, on the other hand, can be magical and much quieter, though days are shorter, many accommodation options and restaurants close up, and the weather is occasionally wild and stormy.

At public holidays and weekends year-round the Cinque Terre receive large numbers of visitors. The Italian public holidays are 1 January (New Year), 6 January (Epiphany), Easter Sunday and Monday, 25 April (Liberation Day), 1 May (Labour Day), 2 June (Republic Day), 15 August (Ferragosto), 1 November (All Saints), 8 December (Immaculate Conception), 25–26 December (Christmas and Boxing Day).

The Cinque Terre are on the whole world's bucket list – and rightly so. So expect crowds in the most popular places. If that bothers you, then plan on visiting in low season, the quietest time, otherwise just get out there and enjoy it!

ACCOMMODATION

The Cinque Terre area is not huge and any one of the villages makes a handy walking base thanks to the excellent train and local bus services. Hotels as such are few and far between due to space restrictions. However there is a wonderful range of accommodation for all pockets. Hostels with shared dormitories and separate rooms can be found in Levanto, Manarola and Porto Venere, otherwise there are countless B&Bs and apartments for rent everywhere. These are a boon for visitors and guarantee an income for local families. However, the flipside is that many inhabitants have moved out to cheaper accommodation in La Spezia so as to rent out their houses to tourists, leading to an inevitable impoverishment of the local fabric and life.

Accommodation is best booked well ahead in high season – namely May and September, as well as Italian public holidays. Of course you can just turn up and try your luck. Knock or ring at the doors with signs for 'rooms for rent' *affittacamere*, *camere*, *stanze* – if they're full they'll send you on to a neighbour or friend. Camping is not allowed anywhere.

Hint: bring as little as possible as rooms are small and you'll inevitably have to drag your bags up and down steep flights of steps yourself – lifts are unheard of. Most railway stations have left luggage facilities.

Be prepared to pay cash for accommodation, unless you've booked online with your credit card or checked beforehand with your host. All the villages have an ATM. Suggestions for places to stay are given in Appendix D. When calling an Italian land line always include the initial '0'. On the other hand numbers beginning with '3' are mobiles and need to be dialled as stand (ie without a zero); the same applies to emergency numbers. When ringing from overseas preface all Italian telephone numbers with +39.

FOOD AND DRINK

Breakfast is rarely provided with accommodation, so do as the locals do and pop out for a fragrant pastry and cappuccino. An increasing number of cafés now serve full breakfast for foreigners with freshly squeezed orange juice, toast and eggs. Grocery shops are plentiful for self-catering.

Typical Ligurian snack food embraces a mouth-watering range of oven-baked pizza and focaccia, known locally as *fugassa*. Soft or crunchy, thick or thin, salt-encrusted or plain, these breads all have a common essential ingredient, the region's delicate olive oil. All manner of toppings are possible – from rosemary, tomato, cheese, greens or whatever

takes the baker's fancy. One traditional variation is tasty *farinata* or *fainà*, flat savoury bread made with chick pea flour. Cheap and nutritious, this may have been introduced by the ancient Romans. These all make delicious picnic fare.

For dinner, first course, unquestionably involving pasta, may be the Genoese speciality *trofie al pesto*, short twirls of fresh pasta with a fragrant sauce of basil leaves, pine nuts, olive oil and parmigiano cheese blended together in a mortar and pestle, or more commonly these days, in a food processor. A traditional addition are green runner beans and chunks of potatoes cooked together with the pasta.

For main courses fish is omnipresent and ranges from freshly grilled or oven baked *branzino* (sea bass) or *orata* (gilthead). More unusual fish the likes of *grongo* (conger eel), *scorfano* (rockfish) and *nasello* (hake) go into a local *zuppa di pesce* stew ever so lightly flavoured with tomato.

Muscoli – the local term for mussels (otherwise called *cozze* in Italian) – come from the Gulf of La Spezia where they have been farmed with great success since 1887. These are sautéed and served either alone or with the delicious addition of *vongole* (clams) and a hint of fresh tomato, often with pasta. Another staple, *acciughe* (anchovies), are on every menu. Glittering silvery fresh and usually perfectly de-boned they are irresistible fried in batter or baked in the *Vernazza*

Zuppa di pesce (fish soup) is a delicious concoction

tegame (casserole dish) with the filleted fish layered with potatoes and tomato. Another Ligurian specialty is *stoccafisso* (dried salted cod) softened and served with mashed potato as *brandacujun*. Cod also comes battered and fried as delicious bite-sized *baccalà fritto*.

On the wine front, all those grapes that walkers admire on the

25

Cinque Terre's steep mountainsides go into some memorable bottles. The best locally produced wines include crisp dry whites. One is Vernaccia from Corniglia, referred to by prominent 14th century poets Boccaccio and Petrarch. With dessert don't miss the sweetish Sciacchetrà passito – bunches of grapes are hung out to dry in the sun to make it.

WHAT TO TAKE

Clothing will depend on the time of year. Generally speaking, in spring–summer (April through to August) T-shirts and shorts are fine, with the addition of a lightweight top. As of autumn (October) and into winter, long trousers and layers of warm garments with the addition of a windproof jacket are essential.

Checklist
- Lightweight walking boots with ankle support are preferable. Quality trainers are also OK as long as they have a good grip and thick soles to protect your feet from loose stones.
- Day pack with a waist belt. Shoulder or hand-held bags are definitely not a good idea as it is safer to have hands and arms free on the trail.
- Rain gear (waterproof jacket and over-trousers, rucksack cover or a poncho).
- One-litre water bottle.

- Swimming costume for coastal routes.
- A compass for following maps.
- Whistle, torch or head-lamp for attracting help in an emergency. Don't rely on your mobile phone as there may not be a signal.
- Trekking poles to help on steep paths.
- Sunglasses, hat and protective cream.
- Basic first aid kit, including plasters and insect repellent.
- Snack food (eg dried fruit or muesli bars) to tide you over if a walk becomes longer than planned.

MAPS

Topographic maps are provided with each route described in this guide. However, commercial maps showing a greater context and landmarks are also very important. The clear 1:25,000 walking map 'Cinque Terre. Porto Venere. Isola Palmaria' published by Consorzio ATI 5 Terre is available at the park visitor centres in the Cinque Terre. It shows all the marked paths.

GPX tracks
GPX tracks for the routes in this guidebook are available to download free at www.cicerone.co.uk/973/GPX. A GPS device is an excellent aid to navigation, but you should also carry a map and compass and know how to use them. GPX files are provided in good faith, but neither the author nor

PATH CLOSURES

Walkers need to be aware that bad weather alerts and risk of rockfall can lead to path closures, as can maintenance work. The local authorities take possible danger very seriously – as should visitors. It is always a good idea to check before setting out on a walk to avoid disappointment – up-to-date information is available at all Cinque Terre information points at the railway stations, as well as www.parconazionale5terre.it/sentieri. Signs warning of closure are posted at the start of a path and walkers must not proceed, tempting as it may be. Anyone who disregards this will be fined. Remember that insurance policies will not cover an accident in such circumstances!

Path closure sign – no entry!

the publisher accept responsibility for their accuracy.

DOS AND DON'TS

Thousands of people from all over the world flock to the Cinque Terre year in year out to walk and enjoy the unique landscapes. But it is essential for each and every visitor to remember that they are just that, visitors, and the need for respect for people, property and the environment is paramount.

- Don't underestimate the Cinque Terre paths. Even though the area is close to the sea it doesn't necessarily mean these are easy strolls. The terrain is rocky, not to mention surprisingly steep in places. Don't be overly ambitious, choose itineraries suited to your ability and study the walk description and map before setting out.

- Wear good quality walking boots or shoes with a non-slip sole. Avoid brand new footwear (beware blisters!). Sandals and flip-flops are totally unsuitable. As the local newspapers bear witness, the emergency services are called in day after day to rescue walkers who have slipped or fallen and twisted or broken an ankle, leg or shoulder, often due to inappropriate footwear.

- Don't set out late on walks even if they're short. Always have extra time up your sleeve to allow for detours and wrong turns. Be aware that in hot weather walking in the middle of the day can lead to sunstroke.
- Don't set out alone, and do tell your accommodation where you'll be walking, as a safety precaution.
- Carry plenty of drinking water and sun protection.
- Don't leave the marked paths.
- Find time to get in decent shape before setting out on your holiday, as it will maximise enjoyment. You'll appreciate the wonderful scenery better if you're not tired, and healthy walkers react better in an emergency.
- Route conditions can change; if in doubt, don't hesitate to turn back and retrace your steps rather than risk getting lost.
- Carry weatherproof and warm gear at all times. Check local weather forecasts and don't start out if rain and storms are forecast, as paths can become slippery if wet and the steep mountainsides and cliffs are subject to rockfalls. In electrical storms, don't shelter under trees or rock overhangs and keep away from metallic fixtures.
- DO NOT rely on your mobile phone as there may not be a signal.
- Please be considerate when making a toilet stop and don't leave unsightly waste lying around as unfortunately far too many walkers do in the Cinque Terre. If you have to use toilet paper or tissues, then take it away – the small plastic bags used by dog owners are perfect.
- Likewise take rubbish away with you. Even organic waste such as apple cores should not be left lying around as it can upset the diet of animals and birds – and spoil things for other visitors. The huge number of visitors on the Cinque Terre paths makes it absolutely essential that everyone follows these basic rules.
- Please don't pick flowers or fruit along the way.
- Remember that the Cinque Terre are in Italy and the local inhabitants shouldn't be expected to speak fluent English. Do make an effort to learn at least basic greetings in Italian: *Buongiorno* (Good morning), *Buona sera* (Good evening), *Arrivederci* (Goodbye) and *Grazie* (Thank you) – rest assured it will be appreciated. More can be found in Appendix D.
- Lastly, don't leave your common sense at home.

Porto Venere's signature church of San Pietro

EMERGENCIES

For medical matters, EU residents need a European Health Insurance Card EHIC. Holders are entitled to free or subsidised emergency treatment in Italy, which has an excellent national health service. UK residents can apply online at www.ehic.org.uk. Australia also has a reciprocal agreement – see www.medicareaustralia.gov.au. Other nationalities need to take out suitable cover. In addition, travel insurance to cover a walking holiday is recommended as rescue and repatriation costs can be hefty.

The following services may be of help should problems arise. No charge is made for these calls.

- Tel 112 for general emergency
- Tel 113 for Polizia (police)
- Tel 118 for health-related urgencies including ambulance (*ambulanza*) and mountain rescue (*soccorso alpino*)
- Tel 1515 to report forest fires
- 'Help!' in Italian is *Aiuto!* pronounced 'eye-you-tow'. *Pericolo* is 'danger'.

Many paths in the Cinque Terre have signposts at regular intervals showing emergency telephone numbers and GPS co-ordinates along with the path number and a reference number. These are invaluable for rescue operations.

USING THIS GUIDE

A total of 16 walks across the Cinque Terre are described in this guide. Visitors wishing to do more should enquire at the park and tourist offices. Each route has been designed to fit into a single day, though for many half a day is enough. About half of the walks here are loop routes so walkers can easily return to their start point; this also means that it is feasible to join in at a different point other than the start if so desired. Cumulative timing is given en route in brackets to make variations possible. Naturally the reverse direction is always an option.

The majority of routes are way-marked with official CAI (Club Alpino Italiano/Italian Alpine Club) red/white paint stripes together with an identifying number found along the way on signposts, prominent stones, trees, walls and rock faces.

Each walk has a heading box containing the following key information about the route:

- **Start** and **Finish**
- **Distance** in kilometres
- **Ascent** and **Descent** This is important information, as height gain and loss are an indication of effort required and need to be taken into account alongside difficulty and distance when planning the day.
- **Grade** Each walk has been classified for difficulty, although adverse weather conditions will make even the simplest route arduous.

  - **Grade 1** – an easy route on clear tracks and paths, suitable for beginners
  - **Grade 2** – paths across hilly terrain, with lots of ups and downs; a reasonable level of fitness is preferable
  - **Grade 3** – strenuous, and possibly with some exposed stretches. Experience and extra care are recommended
- **Walking time** This does not include pauses for picnics, admiring views, photos or nature stops. The 'skeleton' times given are a guide, as each and every walker goes at a different pace and makes an unpredictable number of stops along the way. As a general rule double the times when planning your day and allow for exploratory wanders through the charming villages.
- **Refreshments** Anywhere useful en route. All start and end points have cafés and restaurants as well.
- **Access** Details of how to get to the walk start by public transport or on foot.

In the walk descriptions, useful landmarks that appear on the map are given in bold. Altitude in metres above sea level is given as 'm', not to be confused with minutes, abbreviated as 'min'.

Finally, see Appendix D for an Italian-English glossary which lists common words and expressions that you might come across on maps, signposts or in tourist literature.

WALKS

Vernazza can be admired from the cliff edge on Walk 4

WALK 1

Levanto to Monterosso

Start	Levanto railway station
Finish	Monterosso railway station
Distance	8.5km
Ascent	400m
Descent	400m
Grade	2
Walking time	2hr 45min
Refreshments	Case Lovara
Access	Trains on the La Spezia–Levanto line stop at Levanto and Monterosso.

A marvellously varied traverse across the lofty Punta Mesco headland, this route links Levanto with Monterosso, the first of the Cinque Terre villages, as well as the national park. It also doubles as the opening stage in the memorable multi-day trek from Levanto all the way to Porto Venere. En route here are plenty of vast open views, gardens and woodland. You also pass Case Lovara, a traditional renovated working farmhouse run by FAI, the Italian National Trust, where refreshments, meals and accommodation are on offer (www.poderecaselovara.it).

At the end of the walk, do factor in time for a well-earned swim – there's plenty of free public sand alongside the fee-paying serviced patches with umbrellas and deck chairs.

The path leaves Levanto at the waterfront arches

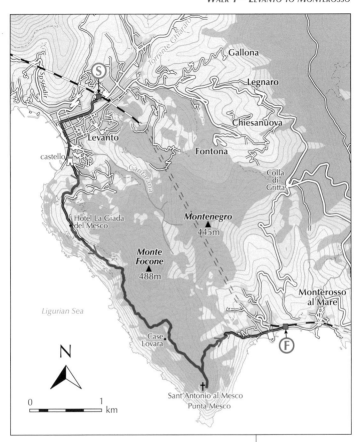

From Levanto railway station go down the stairs and follow the main road as it curves across the **Ghiararo river**.
Continue straight ahead on Corso Roma, seawards. ▶ Just
before the waterfront and Piazza Mazzini, branch L on
Corso Italia along to a park then R under the arches of a
raised road (formerly the railway) where red/white SVA
waymarks appear. These lead past the Casinò Municipale
and a swimming pool and on to the promenade Via

You may like to
detour via the
charming old town
centre – but make
sure you end up
on the seafront
afterwards to pick
up the walk.

33

Gaetano Semenza overlooking the lovely bay. Not far along at some arches don't miss the signed SVA fork L up stepped Salita San Giorgio. It wastes no time climbing past elegant villas to the 13th century **castello**. Go R on the cobbled way S past houses and up into woodland. You join the road for a short stretch as far as **Hotel La Giada del Mesco** for a R turn. This path drops around a panoramic point. A gentle descent through olive groves and orchards sees you approaching **Punta Mesco**, its rugged rocky point plunging into the sea.

As the properties finish, the SVA begins rising through shady holm oak wood on a well graded stepped lane up to a marvellously panoramic stretch through flowering shrubs with stomach-dropping views over the turquoise sea and coves 250 metres below.

The farm property can be visited and refreshments had.

A curve around a side valley sees you at **Case Lovara** (255m, 1hr 40min). ◀ Now a rockier path heads uphill SE, a glorious stretch. You're soon at a junction – go R past an old tower and R again with brilliant views over Monterosso and all the way along the coast to the islands off Porto Venere. Not far on you reach the tiny church of **Sant'Antonio al Mesco** (311m, 20min).

A long-gone monastery was inhabited throughout the 14th century by hermits. It doubled as a watchtower and there's a Second World War bunker to boot. You're high above Punta Mesco and long abandoned quarries where sandstone was once extracted to pave the streets of Monterosso.

Return to the last junction and branch R as the SVA begins its decisive downhill plunge, mostly NE on giant steps that can be knee-testing. A fair way down you tumble out onto the road near Hotel Bellevue and take the tarmac. The path soon resumes before a final bit of road past houses to an easy-to-miss fork R for the final drop past a tower house. Steps wind down overlooking a small harbour to join a concrete lane L past another tower shaded by a magnificent maritime pine. Then it's a stroll

along the seafront of **Monterosso** lined with beach huts and cafés to the **railway station** (12m, 45min).

Admiring the great view over Monterosso

WALK 2
Monterosso via Colla di Gritta circuit

Start/Finish	Monterosso railway station
Distance	11.5km
Ascent/Descent	700m
Grade	2
Walking time	4hr 15min
Refreshments	Colle di Gritta, Santuario di Soviore
Access	Trains on the La Spezia–Levanto line stop at Monterosso. The local ATC bus that links Monterosso Fegina with Colla di Gritta and Santuario di Saviore is handy to vary/shorten the walk.

A wonderful route covering a variety of terrains and landscapes from sand and rock base through marvellous Mediterranean shrubs and maritime pines, chestnut and holm oak. Starting out from the seaside town of Monterosso you climb via a belvedere and abandoned monastery along a marvellously scenic ridge. After a well-located sanctuary, ancient paved ways and knee-testing paths return to the coast. The 'bad' news comes in the form of several rather steep sections, but the good news is the peace and quiet as it doesn't see anywhere as many walkers as other routes.

These steps see you puffing up through flourishing Mediterranean wood with plenty of scenic breaks over the coast and terraced hinterland.

From Monterosso railway station (12m) exit to the sea-front and turn R (W) along the promenade past inviting beaches, cafés and shops. At the **Fegina** junction and bus stop, SVA signposts point you straight ahead, soon uphill past a magnificent maritime pine and tower to the start of steps. These emerge on a quiet road lined with houses to where the path resumes. A final short stretch of tarmac passes the turn-off to Hotel Bellevue (129m) to embark on a near-vertical flight of never-ending steps. ◄ Not far after a welcome bench is the junction for the short detour L past a superb lookout over the Monterosso bay, to **Sant'Antonio al Mesco** (304m, 1hr).

A long-abandoned church is all that's left of a monastery inhabited through the 14th century by hermits. A signal station once operated on the point too and there's also a Second World War bunker.

Back at the junction go L (N) on n.591 uphill, soon past a fork L for Levanto, and continue gently uphill along the lightly wooded ridge on a pleasant sandy path. Another branch L is ignored before you enter dense wood cutting a mountain flank NE to emerge at the gravely saddle and junction **Colla dei Bagari** (360m) with views down to Levanto. Don't turn L but stick with path n.591 rising NE over open terrain with dark green volcanic

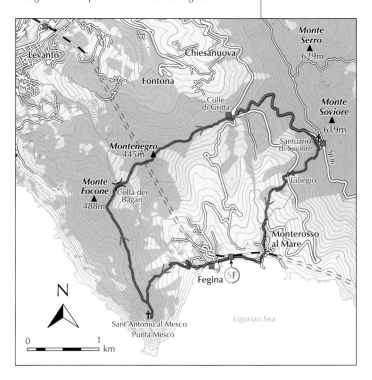

The steep climb from Monterosso

serpentinite rock, passing two radio masts. After a dip comes a climb through pines and tree heather to a well-placed picnic table on **Montenegro** (445m).

A long descent with potentially slippery stretches sees you pass a turn-off for Madonna del Soccorso before a series of ups and downs that conclude happily at the road pass **Colla di Gritta** (330m, 1hr 30min). ▶

Follow red/white waymarks onto the minor road winding up 2.2km to the bus stop then **Santuario di Soviore** (465m, 25min) church and porticoed building with a café-restaurant.

Café-restaurant, hotel, bus stop. If it's handy, by all means ride the bus to Santuario di Soviore or bail out here and return to Monterosso if desired.

Porticoed Santuario di Soviore

Once an important stopover for pilgrims, not to mention a hospital during the 1348 plague, its name is derived from the Latin for 'under the way' referring to an ancient route. Benches appreciated by walkers are shaded by magnificent ancient holm oaks, and there is drinking water, making this a perfect picnic spot.

Alongside the church the old paved way lined with cypresses branches R in decisive descent into chestnut wood, past a derelict chapel. Further on the road is crossed at **Ciliegio** (264m) and a narrower path leads past olive trees to join a concrete lane. A steep stony path takes over on the last stretch, finally emerging on the road close to a car park and roundabout. Walk straight ahead into the village on Via Roma through to Piazza Garibaldi and under the railway arches to the seafront. Turn R off the road (to a tunnel) onto the stepped way with red/white waymarks to the prominent Torre Aurora and on to join the seafront road to the **Monterosso railway station** (1hr 20min).

WALK 3

Monterosso to Vernazza via the sanctuaries

Start	Monterosso railway station
Finish	Vernazza railway station
Distance	9km
Ascent	600m
Descent	600m
Grade	2
Walking time	3hr 40min
Refreshments	Santuario di Soviore, Santuario di Reggio
Access	Trains on the La Spezia–Levanto line stop at Monterosso and Vernazza. At the start, an ATC bus from the roundabout at Monterosso up to Santuario di Soviore means cheating a bit and cutting 1hr 20min off the walk.

While it is long, this rewarding walk joins two of the Cinque Terre's famous coastal villages, Monterosso and Vernazza. It takes a circuitous route that climbs 500 metres high above the coastline to visit two atmospheric sanctuaries. Both the outward leg and the final descent follow age-old pilgrim ways that are both paved and perfectly graded, while the middle section is a delightful contour through bushland thick with scented Mediterranean species.

From Monterosso railway station (12m) stroll L (E) along attractive seafront Via Fegina – trying not to be tempted by the aquamarine water, yellow sand and deck chairs backed by the lovely sweep of the bay. Where the road bears L into a short tunnel, branch R (red/white SVA waymarks) past the old tower Torre Aurora and down to join the road. Go under the railway arches to **Piazza Garibaldi**, a pretty spot with outdoor cafés. Proceed straight ahead (N), keeping to the R of a porticoed building and along pedestrian Via Roma, passing Ristorante Moretto as you head through the old part of the village. ▶ Further up at

The delightful shady way is lined with shops, eateries and hotels.

Piazza Garibaldi in Monterosso

Breaks in the trees mean lovely coastal views, Monterosso included.

a roundabout (20min) with a tourist office, look for the sign and red/white markers that point L to a stepped path, n.509. Climbing steadily the paved way quickly passes B&B Casa dei Limoni, rising into chestnut wood thick with tree heather, broom and extensive wild boar diggings. A stretch of concreted lane takes over before the old paving resumes at a well-marked fork L.

After an olive grove you cross the road at **Ciliegio** (264m). The old way resumes on the opposite side, rising with a steady gradient through pine and chestnut. ◄ A crumbling chapel precedes the final curve for a cypress-lined avenue to the splendid porticoed **Santuario di Soviore** (465m, 1hr 20min).

Santuario di Soviore was once an important stopover for pilgrims, not to mention a hospital during
the 1348 plague. The name is derived from the
Latin for 'under the way' referring to an ancient
route. Café-restaurant, drinking water, bus stop at
the nearby road.

From here you need n.591 R (SSE) past the church
and out of the sanctuary premises to where tarmac leads
up to the Vernazza–Pignone road. Turn R with care for 10
scenic minutes before branching abruptly R at **Termini**
(534m) on well signed n.582. The clear path contours SSE
through flourishing Mediterranean bushes with heaps of
opportunities for admiring the sea and Monterosso well
below now.

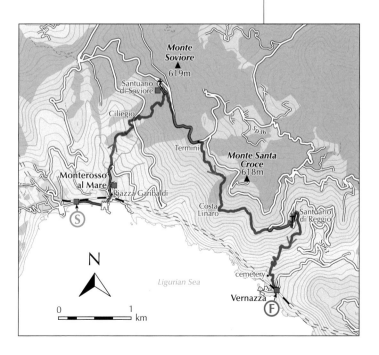

You get amazing views of Vernazza from the path

A short but steep drop – watch your step! – concludes at **Costa Linaro** (404m) with a ruined building and views all the way down the coast to Manarola and Corniglia too. Not far around at a minor road keep R on the tarmac past a vineyard to a signed turn-off for n.508, a lane down to the church and tranquil position of **Santuario di Reggio** (320m, 1hr 20min). ◄

Picnic area, café, drinking water and views over cultivated terraces and hamlets.

A shady avenue leads to the sanctuary gate where you fork R, still on n.508. A marvellous wide paved way descends gently S through light woodland with gorgeous views. This is definitely the most perfectly graded route in the whole of the Cinque Terre.

Further down are the cultivated terraces of Vernazza with vegetables, citrus and grapes.

◄ As you reach the bus stop and **cemetery** the way is concreted as far as the start of the old fortified walls. Don't miss the branch R for steps following the old masonry. At an ancient arch, red/white markings point you L then immediately R for steps past a children's playground and houses to the railway station of **Vernazza** (60m, 40min). But don't end your walk here – continue downhill to the marvellous seafront and harbour.

WALK 4

Monterosso to Vernazza on the SVA

Start	Monterosso railway station
Finish	Vernazza railway station
Distance	4.5km
Ascent	340m
Descent	340m
Grade	2
Walking time	1hr 50min
Refreshments	None
Access	Trains on the La Spezia–Levanto line stop at Monterosso and Vernazza

A simply wonderful walk that while not long, does entail some stiff, knee-challenging flights of steps at the beginning and end (well this is the Cinque Terre…) while the central part means walking hundreds of dizzy metres directly above sheer cliffs and the turquoise sea – thankfully shielded by bushes and trees. As a fitting conclusion, enjoy a swim off the rocks at Vernazza harbour.

Note: this is a fee-paying path; there's a park check point 20min in where tickets are sold and Cinque Terre passes checked.

The beachfront at Monterosso where the walk begins

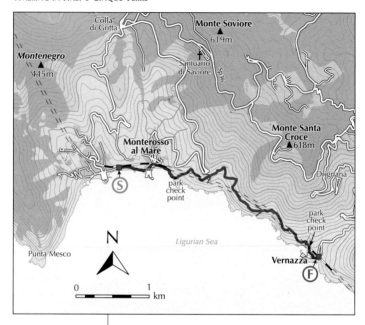

From Monterosso railway station (12m) turn L (E) to stroll along the attractive seafront Via Fegina – trying not to be tempted by the aquamarine water, yellow sand and sun beds. Where the road bears L into a short tunnel, branch R (red/white SVA waymarks) up past the old tower Torre Aurora and down to rejoin the road. Without going under the arches of the raised railway line, keep R past more inviting beaches. A concreted lane leads up towards the entrance to Hotel Porto Roca where you're pointed R onto a spectacular pedestrian walkway hanging off the cliff edge. Steps then take you up to the **park check point** (20min) where fees need to be paid or passes inspected, and loins girded.

Initially you cross a stream and follow its banks through terraced vineyards and gardens served by characteristic Cinque Terre monorails. But soon the stiff climbs start in earnest on a long string of near-vertical staircases between stone walls. ▶ These finally conclude on a marvellous level section where you bid a final *arrivederci* to Monterosso. Around the corner, shady holm oak wood awaits and the first thrilling view to Vernazza. After abandoned terracing and a tiny house you wind in and out of side valleys and cross a slender ancient bridge. Further along is a cat colony, then a bridged stream and derelict building. The descent is steady now, in the company of a monorail and stone walls, as the attractive pastel coloured houses of **Vernazza** appear closer and closer. Vegetable gardens and vineyards announce the proximity of civilisation as does a stunning viewpoint over the harbour and church. After the **park check point** the SVA enters the village and goes clattering down its steep narrow characteristic alleys past slender buildings. You suddenly end up in a river of people on the main street of **Vernazza**. Turn L for the **railway station** (60m, 1hr 30min).

However, it would be unforgiveable to leave without walking down to the charming waterfront and Piazza Marconi where cafés and the church of Santa Margherita d'Antiochia are reflected in the transparent aquamarine waters of the marvellous bay.

Single file is advisable to let oncoming walkers pass.

There are wonderful swathes of green along the way

This spectacular section towards the end of Walk 4 overlooks Vernazza

WALK 5

Vernazza to Corniglia on the SVA

Start	Vernazza railway station
Finish	Corniglia railway station
Distance	4.5km
Ascent	300m
Descent	270m
Grade	2
Walking time	1hr 50min
Refreshments	Prevo
Access	Trains on the La Spezia–Levanto line stop at Vernazza and Corniglia. Near the end, from the village of Corniglia a bus runs down to the railway station, saving 20min.

While not excessively long, this superb walk on the SVA Sentiero Verde Azzurro, will take a good half day by the time you've wandered through the two main villages and stopped repeatedly en route to admire the breathtaking views. Peaceful Corniglia, the destination, is the sole village of the Cinque Terre not directly on the sea – its railway station is located a good 50 metres downhill. The tiny hamlet of Prevo, halfway along, offers refreshments with a view, as well as accommodation should you be interested in getting away from it all.

Be aware that the start and finish sections both entail steep climbs on paths and steps, straightforward in good conditions, though quite slippery in the wet.

Note: Vernazza to Corniglia is one of the Cinque Terre Park's fee-paying pathways so be prepared to buy a day ticket if you don't have a Cinque Terre card.

From Vernazza railway station (60m) head downhill on the main street past the photographic poster showing the 2011 flood devastation. After about 200m at a pharmacy turn sharp L up the stepped way signed red/white 'Sentiero per Corniglia'. Passing Trattoria da Piva the SVA threads its way

These are still planted with olives and fruit trees, soon replaced by holm oak wood and abandoned citrus. Stands of prickly pear and agave punctuate the way.

Its claim to fame is as the halfway mark, a lovely spot to enjoy a rest with a cool drink.

up narrow alleys lined with slim houses, to gain a superb panoramic point over the jagged Vernazza headland complete with old watch tower. Vegetable gardens and orchards precede the **park check point** where fees need to be paid or passes inspected. It is set alongside smooth rock slabs enlivened by red valerian and common rue. Then a mostly level section SE rambles high over the divine sea following lines of ancient terracing. ◄

A steady climb leads past cages of stones, alias retaining walls and sturdy **steel nets** to contain rockfalls and protect the railway line far below. From here it's up and up to the cosy houses and family-run café at the minuscule hamlet of **Prevo** (210m, 45min), hanging onto a cliff miles from anywhere. ◄

Now with gorgeous views to Corniglia on its headland perch, the path embarks on a series of steep drops around a wilder valley, and past a fork R for Guvana

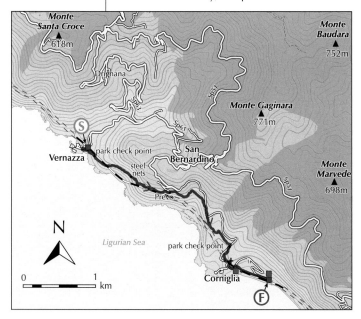

beach. Picnic tables under shady aged olive trees stand directly below the mountain village of **San Bernardino**. Not far along, a miniature stone bridge crosses a side stream and tall stone walls accompany the paved path through jungle-like vegetation to Ponte del Canale, a bridge over Rio della Groppa. Only metres away now is the **park check point**. Here you cross the road for a narrow path through vineyards and houses to a junction near a Romanesque church. Turn R down Via Fieschi to the tiny square of **Corniglia** (84m, 45min) with shops, cafés, ATC bus to the station.

Not far from the start, the path climbs to a marvellous panoramic point overlooking the southern side of Vernazza

Take time out to continue along the main street through the charming old traffic-free heart of the

You cross Ponte del Canale just before reaching Corniglia

village, perched on an impossible promontory. Don't miss the stunning lookout terrace high over the sea.

Back at the square, turn up the road to where the pedestrian route Scalinata Lardarina takes the plunge R. A marvellous series of 33 brick ramps and 382 steps madly zigzags down the steep hillside past lemon gardens. At the bottom, follow the train line to **Corniglia railway station** (30m, 20min).

WALK 6

*Corniglia via Cigoletta and San
Bernardino to Vernazza*

Start	Corniglia railway station
Finish	Vernazza railway station
Distance	7.5km
Ascent	600m
Descent	630m
Grade	2–3
Walking time	3hr 30min
Refreshments	San Bernardino
Access	Trains on the La Spezia–Levanto line stop at Corniglia and Vernazza. The ATC bus between San Bernardino and Vernazza is handy at the end.

A tough but simply spectacular route that climbs high over the coast to the main ridge at 611m above sea level. The upper sections see few walkers. A long descent drops in at the lofty village of San Bernardino, a renowned belvedere over the Cinque Terre villages and coast. The saint in question hailed from the Tuscan city of Siena and reportedly dropped in here in 1485 on his peregrinations.

Be aware that the descent after San Bernardino is extremely steep and can feel exposed – trekking poles will be appreciated! Avoid this concluding section in anything but good stable weather as it has the potential to be dangerous. The local bus to Vernazza offers a straightforward alternative.

Lastly, fit visitors can transform this walk into a superbly rewarding circuit by beginning with the Vernazza–Corniglia traverse described in Walk 5, then picking up this walk at Corniglia for the return – a grand total of 4hr 40min.

From Corniglia railway station (30m) follow signs for the pedestrian route alongside the train lines to the start of the 382 steps and 33 brick ramps of the Scalinata Lardarina that zigzags madly up the steep hillside past lemon gardens. Where it ends at the roadside and Via della Stazione at **Corniglia** (84m, 20min), cross straight over for a lane past houses. Not far up at a prominent junction branch sharp R on n.587 signed for Cigoletta. The old paved way wastes no time gaining height, quickly leaving the village behind on its steady climb NE through vegetable gardens and light wood. ◄ You'll eventually reach the **340m fork** (45min) where n.586 veers R for Volastra and Manarola – ignore this and take the L branch (still n.587), heaps quieter now.

When you stop to get your breath back don't forget to admire the ever-improving views of Corniglia below.

A steady uphill gradient continues through cool shady chestnut wood to a road where you turn L (N) for 300m on the level with views to San Bernardino and all the way to Punta Mesco. Don't miss the narrow path turn-off R resuming the climb in holm oak, the ground messy with boar diggings. A string of modest timber bridges lead

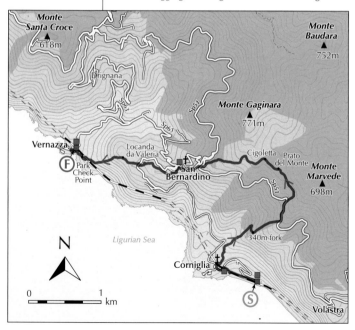

*In the forest
approaching Cigoletta*

around corners and before you know it you emerge at the bracken-infested clearing of **Prato del Monte** (611m) on the main ridge. Turn L (NW) in common with the AV5T (Alta Via Cinque Terre) route for the final level minutes to key junction **Cigoletta** (611m, 45min).

You now need n.507 that soon parts ways with the AV5T proceeding W as a wide track descending through shady holm oak wood. Watch your step on the steep stony sections. ▶ A minor road leads down past houses and you need to keep your eyes peeled for signposts as the path cuts through the many crazy hairpin bends of the road.

As the trees thin, rock roses and scented broom abound, as do coastal views.

Well-tended gardens on the outskirts of San Bernardino

Take your time and enjoy the vast, mesmerising outlook taking in Manarola and Corniglia, as well as distant Monterosso.

Finally, down at 330m is the landmark church and village of **San Bernardino** (40min) along with a belvedere terrace, café and ATC bus stop. Miles and metres away from the coastal bustle.

The following section has few waymarks and concludes with a very steep descent which feels exposed. If in doubt, catch the bus down to Vernazza.

From the **church** take the steps up past houses to an easy-to-miss fork R onto a surprisingly narrow but scenic path NW through terraced fields. About 15min on, at an unmarked T-junction, branch R and soon L to a house where steps drop to the roadside. Cross over and take the dirt road for **Locanda da Valeria**, high over the sea. Just before you reach the actual building, path n.507 forks off L as does a monorail that soon veers off into a field, parting company with walkers. You quickly find yourself plunging down a sun-scorched shoulder and past a hut. ▶ Take extra care on the loose stones. The gradient does ease a little further down as you pass a fenced property before you stagger out to join the busy SVA at last. Here it's R past a **park check point** and a breathtaking lookout over **Vernazza** before waymarks point the way through the maze of tiny alleys and staircases under slim houses. You are deposited in the middle of the flow of visitors in the main street of fascinating Vernazza. Turn R for the **railway station** (60m, 1hr).

Amazing, dizzying views, near-vertical vineyards and challenged knees are the flavour of the afternoon.

Do, however, allow time to visit relaxing Piazza Marconi on the lovely waterfront with its photogenic church. Perhaps you could even fit in a swim?

The walk destination of Vernazza is an awfully long way downhill

WALK 7
Corniglia via Volastra to Manarola

Start	Corniglia railway station
Finish	Manarola railway station
Distance	7km
Ascent	550m
Descent	550m
Grade	2
Walking time	3hr 20min
Refreshments	Volastra
Access	Trains on the La Spezia–Levanto line stop at Corniglia and Manarola

Despite the hefty height gain and loss, this superb panoramic traverse never fails to take visitors' breath away. The well-marked route entails plenty of steep ascent on old paved ways, before running dizzily high over the dramatic coast and sea on narrow paths contouring through ancient terraces and vineyards, witness to the resourceful hard work of the local people. A final long stepped descent concludes at marvellous Manarola.

To help a little there's a bus service at Corniglia from the railway station up to Volastra if you prefer a hand with the ascent, while another links Volastra to Manarola at the end to avoid the steep drop.

From Corniglia railway station (30m) follow signs for the pedestrian route alongside the lines to the start of the 382 steps of the Scalinata Lardarina, a marvellous series of bricked ramps madly zigzagging up the steep hillside past lemon gardens. Where it ends at the roadside Via della Stazione at **Corniglia** (84m, 20min) cross straight over for a lane past houses. Soon, at a prominent junction branch sharp R on n.587. The old paved way wastes no time gaining height, quickly leaving the village behind on its climb NE through vegetable gardens and light wood. ◀ You'll eventually reach the marked **340m**

When you stop to get your breath back don't forget to admire the ever-improving views of Corniglia below.

The Scalinata Lardarina at Corniglia

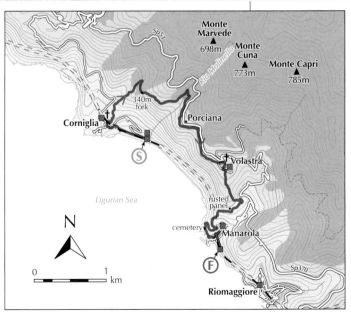

fork where you ignore the L branch for Cigoletta and keep R on n.586. You'll be pleased to know that the bulk of the climb is behind you now and the gradient eases decisively. Now it's mostly E through woodland to cross the valley with the mountain stream Rio Molinello. Not far S are orchards and the modest houses of **Porciana** (380m).

Now a well-signed, marvellous scenic traverse SE coasts below the road overlooking Corniglia and Manarola, though you may be more interested in the immaculately terraced vineyards closer at hand. Take your time here and watch your step on the protruding wires and knobbly branches of the low vines, and of course restrain yourself from picking fruit! The delightful path concludes at the 13th century grey stone **church of Volastra** (336m, 1hr 45min) where benches beckon for a well-deserved rest. ◀

Walk straight out to the road here if you need the bus stop.

> It is believed that a settlement was here in Roman times as a staging post for an ancient coastal route. Nowadays, only 50 people call Volastra home. The name derives from 'village of olives'.

Follow red/white waymarks down via a café-restaurant and L past coloured houses along to a grocery shop on a corner at a junction with drinking water. Brace yourself for the descent, which begins by turning R here as n.506. The pleasant well-graded stepped way – which could also be described as never-ending steep flights of stone steps – heads S in wide curves through well-kept olive groves and light woodland. Just after a small stone house and before the road, take the fork R for 'Manarola panoramica'. (This is slightly longer than the main route via the road, but immensely more panoramic!)

Squeezing past flourishing bushes of tree heather and overlooking vineyards, it contours SW. ◀ After a giant **rusted panel** come stunning views down to the village and the sea. Tiny store huts are dotted along the way in the company of a curious monorail track used for transport during the grape harvest.

Take care not to trip on protruding roots as you proceed along the old stone terraces.

The concluding walkway into marvellous Manarola

The path gradient steepens noticeably as you descend a superbly scenic ridge high over dizzy cliffs and the sea. Watch your step on the loose stones.

Down at old scaffolding (used for a gigantic nativity scene illuminated at Christmas time) especially high steps navigate terraces, with the pastel houses of **Manarola** below. Soon at a T-junction turn R past benches. The panoramic path swings through cultivated terraces before heading downhill past the **cemetery**. Unless you're tempted by the al fresco café and public WC (to your R on the promontory), keep L for the picture-postcard marina at the foot of the cliffs where the houses seem to sprout from the rock. Do find time for an exploratory wander along the lower waterfront promenade and the tiny port. In warm, calm weather swimming is definitely on the cards.

Afterwards, stroll up to the main street Via Discovolo then fork R for the pedestrian tunnel to **Manarola's railway station** (1hr 15min).

WALK 8
Manarola panoramic loop

Start/Finish	Manarola railway station
Distance	3.5km
Ascent/Descent	250m
Grade	2
Walking time	1hr 30min
Refreshments	None
Access	Trains on the La Spezia–Levanto line stop at Manarola

This straightforward yet superbly panoramic loop climbs out of picturesque Manarola to visit vineyards on man-made terraces high on steep hillsides. Walkers enjoy view after stunning view of the rugged coast before looping back down to return to the seafront. It's sobering when you think that the local people use these paths to access their crops.

From Manarola railway station (20m) walk all the way through the pedestrian tunnel to its end at Via Discovolo. Here red/white waymarks for n.506 point you R (NE) uphill past shops and restaurants then an old mill. After Hotel Ca' Andrean turn R up stepped way Via Cozzani to a square containing the **church of San Lorenzo**, close to the youth hostel. Now you need to follow a narrow surfaced road that runs parallel to the Rio Groppo watercourse to a car park. Soon after that, waymarks point you R across the stream and up to another car park. There, paved steps take over on an old way through vegetable gardens and up to cross the road. The tarmac is rejoined briefly for the last time over a bridge to where n.506 branches L (S) as a well-kept stepped pedestrian way that climbs to Volastra. Not far up, just before a tiny stone house, don't miss the signed fork L for 'Manarola panoramica' (45min).

Take care not to trip on protruding roots as you proceed along the old stone terraces.

Squeezing past flourishing bushes of tree heather and overlooking vineyards it contours SW. ◄ After a giant **rusted panel** come stunning views down to the village and the sea.

Tiny store huts are dotted along the way in the company of the curious raised monorail tracks used for transport during the grape harvest.

The path gradient steepens noticeably as you descend a superbly scenic ridge high over dizzy cliffs and the sea. Watch your step on the loose stones.

Map for this route at 1:25,000.

Down at old scaffolding (used for a gigantic nativity scene illuminated at Christmas time, as well as Easter

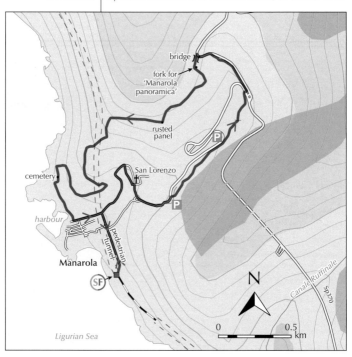

and August festivities) especially high steps drop through terraces. Soon at a T-junction above the pastel houses of **Manarola**, turn R past benches. The panoramic path swings through cultivated terraces before heading down-hill past the cemetery. Unless you're tempted by the al fresco café and public WC (to your R on the promontory), keep L for the picture-postcard marina at the foot of the cliffs where the houses seem to sprout from the rock.

Do find time for an exploratory wander along the lower waterfront promenade and the tiny harbour. Swimming is definitely feasible here. Afterwards, stroll up to the main street then fork R for the tunnel back to **Manarola railway station** (45min).

The dizzy path runs close to the cliff edge

WALK 9
Manarola to Riomaggiore on Via Beccara

Start	Manarola railway station
Finish	Riomaggiore railway station
Distance	2km
Ascent	220m
Descent	220m
Grade	2–3
Walking time	1hr 30min
Refreshments	None
Access	Trains on the La Spezia–Levanto line stop at Manarola and Riomaggiore

A mere single kilometre as the seagull flies separates the seafront villages of Manarola and Riomaggiore, but what a kilometre – over a rugged headland with sheer cliffs. This demanding walk takes a remarkably precipitous route cutting through man-made stone terracing, ascending to 240m above sea level on the abrupt ridge of Costa del Corniolo that separates the two. Known as the Via Beccara, the ancient way was used by the local people for centuries – in fact up until the 1920s when the famous seafront Via dell'Amore saw the light of day lower down. It can still come in handy should that be closed – as it was for reconstruction at the time of writing, in the wake of storm damage and landslips. On the other hand the Via Beccara itself is subject to erosion and ongoing maintenance – enquire locally before starting out and allow for minor discrepancies with the description below.

Be aware that the walk rates Grade 2–3 because it is much steeper than most Cinque Terre pathways, both in the up and down sense; this can be experienced as exhilarating or knee-devastating! There are reportedly 620 steps on both sides – trekking poles definitely come in handy.

From Manarola railway station (20m) walk through the pedestrian tunnel out to the main street Via Discovolo. Turn R uphill past a couple of shops and branch R (before the post office) on narrow Via Belvedere. This climbs SW

The Via Beccara traverses the high ridge with Costa del Corniolo

past houses and gardens, to the Alla Porta Rossa accommodation office. Here a short tunnel leads up to **Piazza Castello**, a marvellous viewpoint. Fork L now on delightful stepped way Via Rollandi winding uphill with a lovely outlook over the houses crammed tightly into the steep-sided valley below. As the gradient eases you stroll NE through upper Manarola to where n.531 strikes off R (S) as **Via Beccara**, not far from the roadside.

Now for serious ascent! Narrow but clear, with high steps, it is accompanied by old rows of terracing colonised by Mediterranean bushes, including stands

Map for this route at 1:25,000.

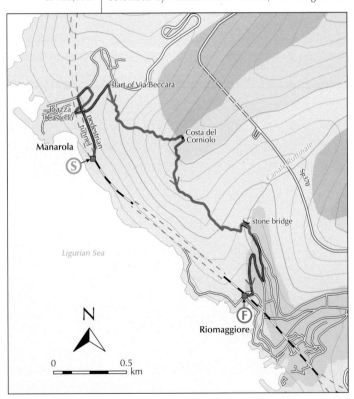

The Via Beccara follows a high crest

of tree heather and scented broom where crops were once planted. The path is aided in many spots by rope handrails. ▸

The reward for all that effort is the stunning ridge-cum-lookout **Costa del Corniolo** (240m, 50min). ▸

Ignore the path turn-off L and prepare for the plunge R (S) on n.531. Initially it touches on a black water tank to where a handrail helps along a stretch with dizzying views. There are not many waymarks so you need to follow the well-trodden way, not the narrow turn-offs to private plots of land with orderly rows of grape vines. Ignore the fork L for path n.531C out to the roadside and continue in descent SE, going slowly on the loose stones. What feels like an especially vertical flight of steps via terraced vegetable gardens concludes near an ancient **stone bridge** crossing Canale Ruffinale among lemon orchards. You're led to where the path forks R to join a road. Not far along n.531 points R onto Via Telemaco Signorini which curves down past houses, finally reaching the railway station of **Riomaggiore** (20m, 40min).

Take your time and watch your step.

From this angle you're almost directly over the pastel houses of Manarola surrounded by extensive terracing. The railway and station are at your feet, seemingly only metres from the rocks and waves. Your destination, Riomaggiore, is out of sight for the moment.

WALK 10
Riomaggiore high circuit

Start/Finish	Riomaggiore railway station
Distance	7.5km
Ascent/Descent	900m
Grade	2
Walking time	3hr
Refreshments	Roadside café below the Santuario
Access	Trains on the La Spezia–Levanto line stop at Riomaggiore

Although it is rather long, this rewarding circuit is both delightfully varied and relatively untrodden. Once the village is left behind, steep stepped paths climb through vineyards and Mediterranean shrubs into dense woodland. Once up at the 400m mark it contours to a brilliantly located sanctuary, easily one of the top rating belvederes on the Cinque Terre. The walk concludes with a scenic, knee-challenging plunge back to Riomaggiore.

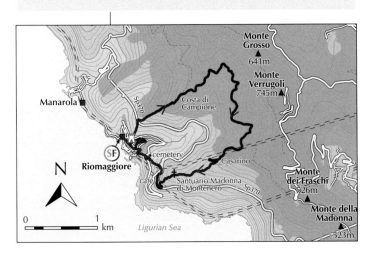

From Riomaggiore railway station (20m) walk all the way through the pedestrian tunnel towards the *centro*. At the end turn L up the main street Via Colombo past shops and eateries. As you reach the public toilets (on the R side of the road), turn L taking a broad flight of steps lined with houses. Keep L again on steeper Scalinata della Valle then next L through to the church and its panoramic square overlooking citrus orchards. Via Pecunia leads on through upper Riomaggiore to the **Castello** (75m).

Here take the steps to a signposted junction where you need n.501 crossing a car park before embarking on a stepped lane. Guided by red/white stripes this heads N away from the village and into vegetable gardens in the company of high dry stone walls and a black water pipe. ▶ After a series of concrete steps, ignore a fork R

The Castello in upper Riomaggiore

Up, up and up best describes it!

71

at a water tank and continue on a level stretch to cross a road not far from a viaduct.

Bearing NE now, the path becomes a little rougher climbing through pocket vineyards with their miniature monorails for the harvest. Wilder vegetation takes over, with tree heather, broom and even the odd pine tree. ◄

Openings spell views to Volastra NW and over the gulf to Monterosso.

Once you've reached the path junction and wide lane at **Costa di Campione** (395m, 1hr) the bulk of the climb is behind you.

The Santuario Madonna di Montenero stands out.

Here branch R on n.530, NE at first. ◄ It's a pleasant stroll through patches of chestnut trees and woodland alive with birdsong, winding in and out of the folds of the mountainside. Further along, a short uphill surfaced stretch leads to **Casarino** (405m) where you branch R. Only minutes downhill ignore the fork L for Telegrafo and follow the route marked SVA to a belvedere with well-placed benches. Continue past modest houses on a fenced path to the gloriously positioned **Santuario Madonna di Montenero** (334m, 1hr 10min). ◄

This perfect picnic spot has a breathtaking outlook that embraces the Ligurian coast from the island of Palmaria to Monterosso, as well as a bird's-eye view of Riomaggiore.

Benches at Santuario Madonna di Montenero invite walkers to drink in the sea views

Never-ending flights of steps take you back to Riomaggiore

At the front of the church, path n.593V begins its enjoyable – if relentless descent into bushes past a pylon. Further down at the roadside, cross over with care – keep R to a **café** with an inviting terrace. Take the next road fork R; it curves back under the main road to where the path resumes immediately. Steps lead down to the village **cemetery** where you cross the road again to pick up the descent path. More flights of steep steps conclude at a children's playground in the residential area. Here you are directed R along Via di Loca, a short-lived level stretch – enjoy it while it lasts – before it's L (red/white markers) for the final near-vertical plunge. This deposits you in the main street, Via Colombo, where a L turn and soon R will see you safely back at the **Riomaggiore railway station** (50min). ▸

However by heading downhill you'll reach the seafront and charming, albeit cramped, old harbour.

WALK 11
Riomaggiore low circuit

Start/Finish	Riomaggiore railway station
Distance	4.5km
Ascent/Descent	420m
Grade	2
Walking time	2hr
Refreshments	Roadside café below the Santuario
Access	Trains on the La Spezia–Levanto line stop at Riomaggiore

This delightful circuit walk is fairly short and straightforward, though the concluding descent can be hard on the knees. At the start, after climbing out of Riomaggiore it embarks on a beautifully graded old paved way up to Santuario Madonna di Montenero, picnic spot and belvedere par excellence with awesome coastal views. Decidedly steep stepped paths waste no time returning to sea level afterwards.

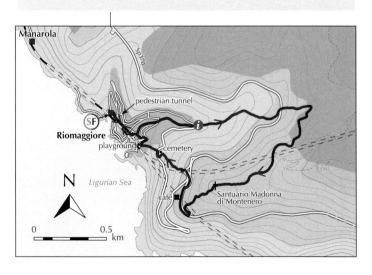

It's a leisurely ascent on the paved lane out of Riomaggiore

▶ From Riomaggiore railway station (20m) walk through the pedestrian tunnel towards the *centro*. At the end turn L up the main street Via Colombo, lined with shops and eateries. Walk all the way up through a string of car parks to a T-junction and information office. Straight across the road near L'Arcobaleno rooms are signs for the SVA. The old cobbled way crosses a tiny stone bridge and climbs gently E, passing tiny houses and terraced plots high above the stream Canale di Riomaggiore. You cross a road near a batch of old crosses and another bridge before steps climb past well-kept vineyards. Accompanied by the occasional votive shrine in light woodland, the way swings S rising effortlessly.

On a marvellously open promontory corner stands gloriously positioned **Santuario Madonna di Montenero** (334m, 1hr 10min). ▶

Once rested, walk to the front of the church for path n.593V and an enjoyable – if relentless – descent into bushes and past a pylon. Down at the roadside, cross over

Map for this route at 1:25,000.

This beautiful picnic spot has benches and a breathtaking outlook along the Ligurian coast from the island of Palmaria to Monterosso, as well as a bird's-eye view of Riomaggiore.

Santuario Madonna di Montenero is a great spot for a picnic

with care and keep R to a **café** with an inviting terrace. Take the next road fork R; you curve back under the main road to where the path resumes immediately. Steps drop to the village **cemetery** where you cross the road again to pick up the descent path opposite. More flights of steep steps conclude at a children's **playground** in the residential area. Here you are directed R along Via di Loca, a short-lived level stretch – enjoy it while it lasts, as you're soon pointed L (red/white markers) for the final near-vertical plunge between tall houses. This finally deposits you in the main street, Via Colombo, where a L turn and soon R will see you safely back at the Riomaggiore railway station (50min). However by heading downhill you'll reach the seafront and the old harbour.

WALK 12

Riomaggiore to Porto Venere

Start	Riomaggiore railway station
Finish	Porto Venere
Distance	13.5km
Ascent	670m
Descent	700m
Grade	2–3
Walking time	5hr
Refreshments	Colle del Telegrafo, Valico Sant'Antonio, Campiglia
Access	Trains on the La Spezia–Levanto line stop at Riomaggiore. At the end, ATC buses run from Porto Venere to La Spezia if you need a train back to Riomaggiore. Otherwise take a leisurely ferry. To make the day a little shorter, there's an ATC bus from Riomaggiore up to Colle del Telegrafo, and further on a service between Campiglia and La Spezia, should you need to bail out.

This magnificent traverse leads up away from the Cinque Terre coastline to follow superbly scenic ridges before dropping to a wonderful conclusion at utterly charming Porto Venere on the edge of La Spezia gulf. The walk can easily be fitted into a single day, however it is better enjoyed in chunks so it doesn't become a marathon. Campiglia is a lovely spot for a stopover (and more walks).

Walking is straightforward, though be aware that after Campiglia the rocky paths are narrow and have been worn slippery due to the passage of many boots.

From Riomaggiore railway station (20m) walk through the pedestrian tunnel towards the *centro* and at the end turn L up the main street Via Colombo. Continue past shops and eateries all the way up through a string of car parks and a T-junction, information office and a bus stop (for

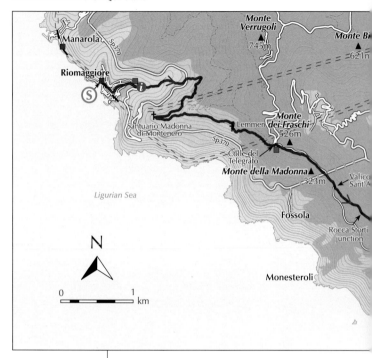

Colle del Telegrafo). Straight across the road near the L'Arcobaleno rooms are signs for the SVA. The old cobbled way crosses a tiny stone bridge and climbs gently E, passing tiny houses and terraced plots high above the stream Canale di Riomaggiore. You cross a road near a batch of old crosses and another bridge before steps climb past well-kept vineyards. Accompanied by the occasional votive shrine in light woodland, the way swings S rising effortlessly.

On a marvellously open promontory corner stands gloriously positioned **Santuario Madonna di Montenero** (334m, 1hr 10min). ◄

Turn uphill on the signed path past gardens and modest houses, to where the SVA veers sharp R. Heading

This perfect picnic spot has benches and a breathtaking outlook that takes in the Ligurian coast from the island of Palmaria to Monterosso, as well as a bird's-eye view of Riomaggiore.

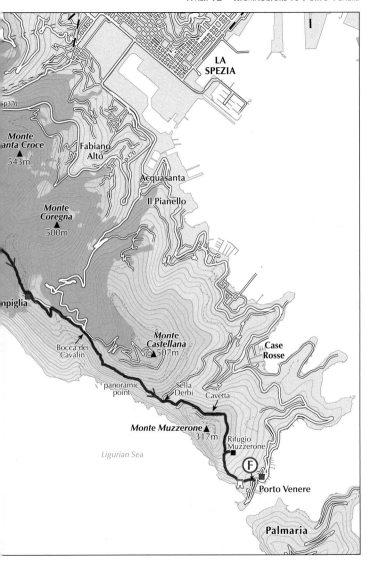

La Spezia

Monte
Santa Croce
▲
543m

Fabiano
Alto

p370

Acquasanta

Il Pianello

Monte
Coregna
▲
500m

Campiglia

Bocca dei
Cavalin

Monte
Castellana
▲ 507m

Case
Rosse

panoramic
point

Sella
Derbi

Cavetta

Monte Muzzerone ▲
317m

Rifugio
Muzzerone

Ligurian Sea

Ⓕ

Porto Venere

Palmaria

E it embarks on a beautiful mostly level traverse in the company of rock roses and yellow broom over terraced vineyards and, of course, the sea. After the handful of houses and tiny 13th century chapel at **Lemmen** the path soon heads up high stone steps via wooded terraces and power lines. In no time at all you're at **Colle del Telegrafo** (515m, 50min). Café-restaurant, bus stop.

Turn R (ESE) in common with red/white waymarked AV5T and 'Palestra nel verde' (a fitness route) on a shady lane that keeps above the road, on the main ridge now. ◄ The road is joined for a short stretch through **Valico Sant'Antonio** (508m) with its welcoming café and picnic tables. Continue straight ahead on a lane uphill SE with drier Mediterranean vegetation and on through the **Rocca Storti junction** (558m). From here on a wide path begins a gentle shady straightforward descent, concluding at the vegetable gardens and houses of laid-back **Campiglia** (403m, 1hr). ◄

Walk on past the church and turn L on red/white marked AV5T skirting a building and side entrance to

The chestnut trees are magnificent here.

Accommodation, cafés, restaurants, groceries, bus to La Spezia. The main square doubles as a marvellous belvedere that even takes in Corsica on clear days.

After Campiglia there are awesome views towards Monte Muzzerone and the island of Palmaria

The final descent to Piazza Bastreri in Porto Venere

friendly Piccolo Blu café. It's not far past an old wind-mill then picnic tables before you veer L to join the road. Follow this downhill past a house then at the next curve turn off R on the clear if unsigned path. Waymarks soon re-appear on trees and over a rise you drop to touch on the road at a saddle **Bocca dei Cavalin** (343m).

High above the sea a clear narrow path continues through tall clumps of grass and over rocky outcrops that need clambering over. ◄ A superbly **panoramic point** below Monte Castellana affords views to the sheer cliffs of Monte Muzzerone with the Porto Venere headland beyond. A long descent touches on a picnic table before concluding at the road and **Sella Derbi** (190m, 1hr).

Follow the tarmac E past the **Cavetta** quarry. ◄ Up at a 246m fork leave the road for the lane straight ahead through shady woodland down to the turn-off L for **Rifugio Muzzerone**.

> A 5min detour will see you at this relaxing spot (refreshments, meals and accommodation) looking out to Palmaria and La Spezia gulf backed by the Alpi Apuane.

From the turn-off continue downhill (S). You're soon joined by a side path (n.516) from Forte Muzzerone near a derelict hut with rusting machinery and hunks of black stone left from quarrying days. The gradient steepens a lot, so do watch your step on the loose stones. Where the path leaves the cover of trees all of a sudden you get fabulous views over Porto Venere, its castle and headland backed by the spread of the island of Palmaria. Down at the foot of the soaring castle walls it's L for a final plunge on a stepped way through thickets of oyster plant, coming to a wonderful conclusion at Piazza Bastreri in beautiful **Porto Venere** (1hr).

Watch your step as it's well worn and can be slippery.

This is one of the remaining three where the prized black marble Portoro has been extracted since ancient Roman times.

WALK 13
Campiglia circuit via Monesteroli and Fossola

Start/Finish	Campiglia
Distance	7.5km
Ascent/Descent	745m
Grade	2–3
Walking time	4hr
Refreshments	Fossola, Valico Sant'Andrea
Access	Campiglia has ATC buses from La Spezia, with connections to Porto Venere. Fossola, an alternative entry point, is on the ATC route from Riomaggiore and the Explora bus from La Spezia also stops there.

This beautiful route explores the relatively little-visited southernmost reaches of the Cinque Terre with cultivated hillsides and ancient vertiginous paths testifying to man's genius and masterly work in creating terracing and stepped pathways on impervious terrain hundreds of metres above the sea. After a lovely jaunt from the scenic village of Campiglia comes the *scala grande* 'great staircase' dropping to Monesteroli. Simply awesome (and rated Grade 3) it is not for the faint of heart or knee – and can be avoided (see below). With around 1100 stone steps it is a masterpiece of civil engineering negotiating an impossibly steep mountainside down to a miniature fishing settlement perched over the sea edge.

Note: be aware that from Monesteroli itself the rest of the way down to the sea is a scramble in the best of conditions, but more often than not it's closed due to landslips – don't take unnecessary risks! (If it's a swim you're after, the beach at Punta Persico in Walk 14 is more suitable.)

Afterwards the walk takes a dizzy scenic traverse to the hillside settlement of Fossola, where access/exit from the nearby road is feasible. An old paved path culminates on the upper ridge for a pleasant return to Campiglia. With the exception of the final section, you'll meet very few other people.

From the word go there are gorgeous views to the sea, as well as the house of Schiara cascading down vine-covered slopes.

From the square at Campiglia (403m) facing the sea, walk R past the café-grocery shop then turn L on n.535 at Locanda Tramonti. The alley heads NW away from the houses and through well-tended gardens. ◄ Following old terracing through woodland you briefly join a minor road near a monorail and after a matter of metres downhill are pointed R. A wide stepped way climbs into cool holm oak wood to **Fontana di Nozzano** (344m).

Used until recently by the local women for their washing, the monumental fountain was built by soldiers of Napoleon in 1805 when they were on the lookout for enemy English ships during a naval blockade.

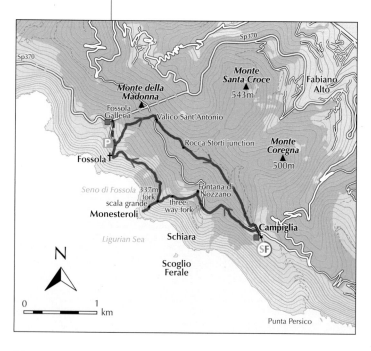

A key path junction for the Monesteroli walk

Here n.535 forks sharp L (W) narrowing and traversing cultivated hillsides. ▸ At a **three-way fork** keep L for the start of the famous *scala grande*. The 'great staircase' certainly lives up to its name. Vertiginous to say the least, it wastes no time in plunging seawards on stone steps with the houses of Monesteroli impossibly below you amid shrubs and vineyards. A second **fork** at 337m (45min) is quickly reached. ▸

Rating Grade 3 difficulty, there are seemingly near-vertical steps that seem to get steeper and steeper and feel exposed, but the views get better and better as you proceed the rest of the winding way down to **Monesteroli** (118m) and its houses-cum-storerooms. ▸

Return to the **337m fork** (1hr 15min) and go L (N) for the narrow path that makes its careful way across the steep wooded hillsides high above Seno di Fossola bay. Picnic tables are encountered, as are clumps of spiky agave and masses of scented curry plant before the first houses, terraced gardens – and (yet more) steps threading in and out, down and up into spread-out **Fossola**. A wide

The pointy offshore rock Scoglio Ferale is at your feet.

Note: if you don't feel comfortable on the staircase then stop here and turn R – pick up the description below.

The unusual place name may owe its origin to Menestheus, a Greek hero and protector of sailors who reputedly founded it with a group of Athenians.

The famous staircase to Monesteroli, which can be seen far below

staircase climbs to the tiny church in a lovely scenic spot, followed by a car park (284m, 40min).

Detour to Fossola Galleria

From here in 5min you can detour L (N) to a café-restaurant, park information point and bus stops on the main road at **Fossola Galleria** (365m), the start of a tunnel. This is a handy alternative entry/exit point.

From the **car park** steps continue steadily uphill (n.534) into woodland with stretches of fencing to keep out wild boars. Before you know it, you're at a minor road and turn R to the picnic area and inviting café at **Valico Sant'Antonio** (508m, 40min) on the main ridge.

Continue straight ahead (SE) on a lane uphill through dry Mediterranean vegetation and on through the **Rocca Storti junction** (558m). From here on the wide path (AV5T) begins a gentle, shady, straightforward descent, concluding at the vegetable gardens and houses of laid-back **Campiglia** (403m, 40min).

WALK 14
Punta Persico

Start/Finish	Campiglia
Distance	3km
Ascent/Descent	400m
Grade	2
Walking time	1hr 45min
Refreshments	None
Access	Campiglia has ATC buses from La Spezia, with connections to Porto Venere.

A well-kept secret in this magical part of the Cinque Terre, is this plunging stepped path from the belvedere village of Campiglia down to the aquamarine water and beach of Punta Persico. En route are precipitous slopes terraced and proudly cultivated by local people almost the whole way down to the sea 400 metres below. A remarkable ongoing feat.

Take swimming gear and plenty of drinking water on the walk. Sandals come in handy for the beach as it has large pebbles. Try to avoid returning uphill in the mid-afternoon heat on a summer's day – remember it's a 400m climb and you'll have the sun beating on your back. After the exertion, treat yourself to a memorable meal with locally grown produce and a view at La Lampara, or a drink with a view at the café in the square, which also does snacks and groceries.

From the square at Campiglia (401m) near the café/shop, turn sharp L (SE) on Via Tramonti, marked as n.528. The stepped lane easily moves downwards, soon passing the restaurant **La Lampara**. The going is step by big stone step, wall after dry stone wall, in the constant company of black water pipes supplying vineyards and olive groves. ▶ A procession of houses in panoramic spots is dotted down the hillside. At the last building around the 100m mark is an ancient **mulberry tree** strapped around

Spontaneous flowering plants like delicate myrtle, red valerian and broom flourish here too.

The sea can be admired the whole way down to Punta Persico

the midriff to prevent splitting, its gnarled branches propped up with iron poles.

Soon the staircase steepens even more as the pull of the turquoise sea proves to be irresistible. Watch your step the rest of the way down to the **beach** on the west side of **Punta Persico** (0m, 45min) for a well-deserved dip.

Return to Campiglia the same way (1hr).

Turquoise water is the reward at Punta Persico beach

Map for this route at 1:25,000.

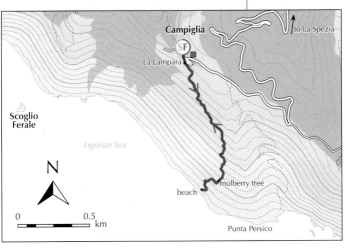

WALK 15
Porto Venere and Monte Muzzerone

Start/Finish	Piazza Bastreri, Porto Venere
Distance	4km
Ascent/Descent	280m
Grade	2
Walking time	1hr 50min
Refreshments	Rifugio Muzzerone
Access	Frequent ATC buses connect La Spezia with Porto Venere, and there are also ferries from spring to October.

This immensely rewarding circuit is a jaunt up Monte Muzzerone, the cliff-cum-mountain that acts as the backdrop for charming Porto Venere. With a promise of magnificent views over the Gulf of La Spezia, it leads through olive groves and woodland before dropping in at a welcoming rustic refuge where drinks and meals, as well as basic accommodation, are available. However, be aware that the concluding descent to Porto Venere is pretty steep.

On the way up, a slightly shorter (1hr 10min) loop is feasible by shortcutting to Rifugio Muzzerone at the 164m junction.

With a capacity for 600 people, they date back to 1942 to protect civilians from Allied bombings, in view of the vicinity of the naval base at La Spezia.

In Piazza Bastreri, the main square of Porto Venere (15m), directly opposite Hotel Genio is a WW1 cenotaph and a plaque paying homage to the victims of quarry accidents. To its immediate R are public toilets and the entrance to Second World War air raid shelters. ◄ Here signs point R for n.519 and **Rifugio Muzzerone**. The steadily stepped way wastes no time in ascending N through the residential area and onto a rougher stony path enclosed by dry stone walls. As you bear NW olive trees are constant companions as well as the occasional modest house. Moreover with every step taken in ascent the views improve back over Porto Venere, the island of Palmaria and the gulf.

MONTE MUZZERONE

Monte Muzzerone has been quarried since ancient Roman times for the black marble Portoro, prized for its brilliant veins of gold. As late as 1862 there were still 30 working quarries on its slopes – down to three nowadays, and undergound for the most part. Woodland has all but submerged the abandoned works, with the odd piece of rusting machinery peeking through. These days the Muzzerone's sheer sea cliffs are a magnet for intrepid climbers.

At a signed **164m fork** (20min) the bulk of the climb is behind you now. Unless you short cut straight ahead to Rifugio Muzzerone (10min away), go R on n.517. This means a relaxing contour N along olive terraces and woodland where the soil has been dug up extensively by wild boar in their quest for food. At a **four-way junction** (191m) keep straight ahead then not far along make sure you branch sharp L uphill on n.516/517 and soon R again

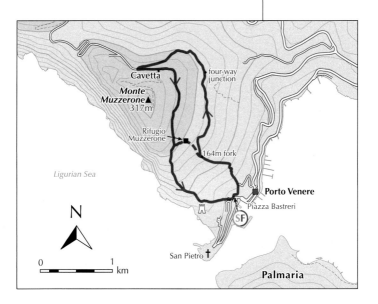

91

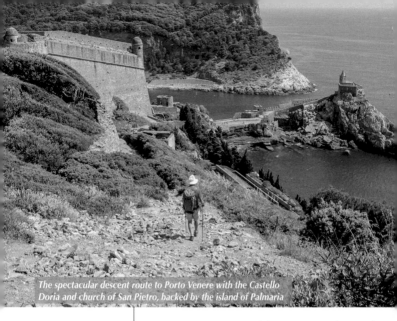

The spectacular descent route to Porto Venere with the Castello Doria and church of San Pietro, backed by the island of Palmaria

(W) on n.517. Limestone slabs are traversed in gentle ascent to a rough surfaced road.

Turn L in company with the AVG (Alta Via del Golfo) for a gentle uphill stretch past the **Cavetta** quarry to the turn-off (246m) where a signed lane leaves the tarmac for a short ramble through woodland to a fork down L for nearby **Rifugio Muzzerone** (200m, 50min). ◄

Return to the main path and turn L (S), soon in descent. A side path (n.516) from higher Forte Muzzerone joins up near a derelict hut with rusting machinery and hunks of black rock left from the days of quarrying. The gradient steepens a lot, so do watch your step on the loose stones. Where the path leaves the cover of trees you enjoy a fabulous outlook down to **Porto Venere**, its castle and headland backed by the spread of the island of Palmaria. Further down at the foot of the soaring castle walls it's L for a final plunge on a stepped way that concludes back at **Piazza Bastreri** (40min).

A drink or meal on the shady terrace will give you time to enjoy the marvellous views over the gulf backed by the marble-white Alpi Apuane.

WALK 16
Palmaria island circuit

Start/Finish	Terrizzo
Distance	6km
Ascent/Descent	300m
Grade	2–3
Walking time	2hr 30min + 30min for return ferry trip from Porto Venere
Refreshments	Terrizzo, Pozzale (summer only)
Access	Frequent buses connect La Spezia with Porto Venere, as do ferries from spring to October. From Porto Venere a year-round local ferry covers the short distance to the neighbouring island of Palmaria, depositing visitors at Terrizzo.

The modest island of Palmaria is essentially a huge lump of rock and woodland off Porto Venere. It was once of great strategic military importance due to its vicinity to the huge naval port of La Spezia and is dotted with forts and installations dating from the 1860s up to the Second World War; it reputedly once had more than 500 cannons. Palmaria was also a veritable treasure trove of stone: first and foremost of limestone that went into the massive mid-1800s defensive breakwater barrier constructed across the Gulf of La Spezia.

Along with abandoned quarries and old forts, the island features flourishing olive groves, droves of wandering goats, rabbits and raucous colonies of herring gulls. These days a mere handful of residents call the island home; however, evidence has been unearthed of Neolithic settlement (c.5000 years ago) in caves on the rugged west coast. These led to the name Palmaria – from the Celtic-Ligurian dialect *balme* for caves. Last on the list of curiosities: the island was used a set for the 1961 film *The Guns of Navarone*. Quite a mixture!

This sets the stage for the worthwhile walk known as the *Giro dell'Isola* (island circuit) as it circumnavigates the island visiting beaches and dramatic cliffs. Well marked with red/white paint stripes, it's straightforward walking with a couple of stiff stretches – namely the path towards Pozzale, then the final descent which is steeper, demanding special care. If desired, this can be avoided – see below.

The Palmaria ferry at Porto Venere

At Terrizzo and the renowned restaurant/guesthouse Locanda Lorena are path signposts. Go L (NE) along the waterfront past a bathing establishment to a lane which climbs gently. Keep R at the ensuing fork, rising above an old fort (Umberto I). The way bears S to a picnic table and the cannon emplacements of **Batteria Albini**. Here at the junction keep L (signed for Pozzale) and proceed through olive groves high over **Cala della Fornace** with lovely views over the Gulf of La Spezia. About 5mins along keep R in gentle ascent (unless you choose the longer route L via Punta Mariella) through Mediterranean shrubs including scented myrtle and broom. Stick with this path as it rounds a point with wonderful views over the cove of Pozzale to the island of Tino with its landmark lighthouse.

Further around through terracing, the path begins its somewhat steep descent towards the sea. A handrail helps, but watch your step on the crumbly stretches down to the pebble beach of **Pozzale** (1hr).

Now turn R following signs for '*Vetta*' (summit) past a renowned restaurant and along the seafront at the foot of a long-abandoned quarry, now home to a chaotic colony of herring gulls as well as Aleppo pines. Unless you have extra time up your sleeve to extend S to Capo dell'Isola, take the abrupt fork R. The clear path marked in red/white climbs steadily and decidedly through shady oak wood to a **saddle** (65m) and long-abandoned quarry workings high over the sheer cliffs of **Cala Grande**. A dramatic spot.

A minor road from Terrizzo comes up this far – follow this R downhill if you prefer to avoid the steep descent of the walk route.

The path proceeds N-NW uphill in the company of old stone walls and power poles, tree heather and pine trees, and ever-improving sea views. Picnic tables and a path junction mark the **Vetta** high point (175m, 40min). ▸

Take the lane L below the road, signed for 'Carlo Alberto' (a reference to a long-gone monument to an Italian king) leading NW through to the former Batteria Semaforo radar facility, now the 'Centro Educazione Ambientale'. This is the start of the steep *sentiero difficile*

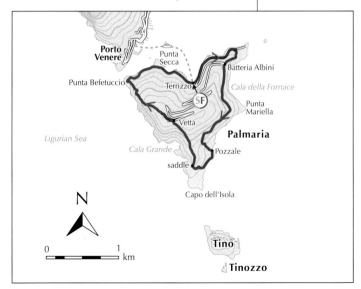

Near the abandoned quarry after Pozzale

(difficult path). Not far along where power poles start, is an amazing view down to Porto Venere and its iconic headland church banked by cliffs. Watch your step in descent, through wood at first but high over the sea. A stretch crosses R under the power line, and is aided with a rope handrail, before continuing its plunging way. You clamber down shallow rock gullies to a superb lookout on **Punta Befettuccio**.

The gradient eases considerably now as you bear NE in the company of domed clumps of tree spurge. As you reach the waterfront, turn R past pebble beaches and houses on **Punta Secca**, then a navy-owned bathing establishment, before the Locanda and **Terrizzo** (50min).

An abandoned quarry over the sheer cliffs of Cala Grande

APPENDIX A
Village maps

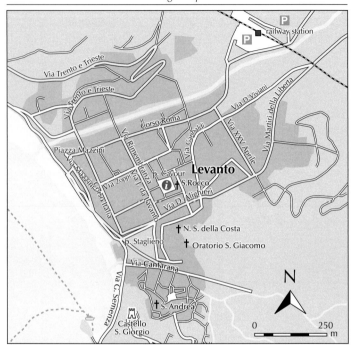

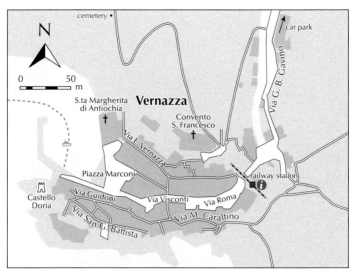

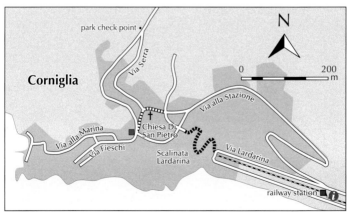

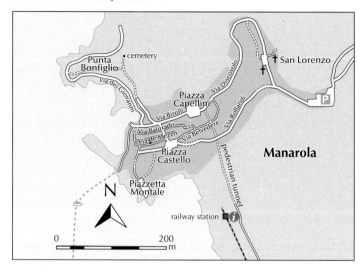

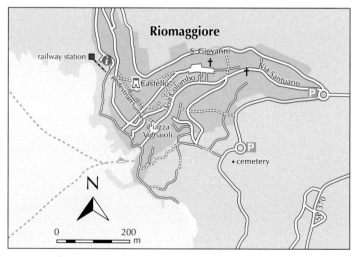

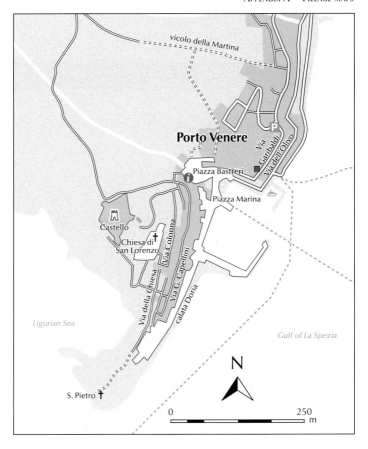

APPENDIX B

Route summary table

Walk	Title	Distance	Ascent/Descent	Grade	Time	Page
1	Levanto to Monterosso	8.5km	400m/400m	2	2hr 45min	32
2	Monterosso via Colla di Gritta circuit	11.5km	700m/700m	2	4hr 15min	36
3	Monterosso to Vernazza via the sanctuaries	9km	600m/600m	2	3hr 40min	41
4	Monterosso to Vernazza on the SVA	4.5km	340m/340m	2	1hr 50min	45
5	Vernazza to Corniglia on the SVA	4.5km	300m/270m	2	1hr 50min	49
6	Corniglia via Cigoletta and San Bernardino to Vernazza	7.5km	600m/630m	2–3	3hr 30min	53
7	Corniglia via Volastra to Manarola	7km	550m/550m	2	3hr 20min	58
8	Manarola panoramic loop	3.5km	250m/250m	2	1hr 30min	63
9	Manarola to Riomaggiore on Via Beccara	2km	220m/220m	2–3	1hr 30min	66
10	Riomaggiore high circuit	7.5km	900m/900m	2	3hr	70
11	Riomaggiore low circuit	4.5km	420m/420m	2	2hr	74
12	Riomaggiore to Porto Venere	13.5km	670m/700m	2–3	5hr	77
13	Campiglia circuit via Monesteroli and Fossano	7.5km	745m/745m	2–3	4hr	83
14	Punta Persico	3km	400m/400m	2	1hr 45min	87
15	Porto Venere and Monte Muzzerone	4km	280m/280m	2	1hr 50min	90
16	Palmaria island circuit	6km	300m/300m	2–3	2hr 30min	93

APPENDIX C

Useful information

Park information points
www.parconazionale5terre.it

Corniglia
tel 0187 812523

La Spezia
tel 0187 743500

Levanto
tel 0187 801312

Manarola
tel 0187 760511

Monterosso
tel 0187 817059

Riomaggiore
tel 0187 920633 or 0187 760091

Vernazza
tel 0187 812533

Porto Venere
tel 0187 794823
www.parconaturaleportovenere.it

Tourist Offices
La Spezia
tel 0187 026152
www.myspezia.it

Levanto
tel 0187 808125
www.visitlevanto.it

Monterosso
tel 0187 817506
www.prolocomonterosso.it

Porto Venere
tel 0187 790691
www.prolocoportovenere.it

Riomaggiore
tel 0187 762271

Vernazza
www.visitvernazza.org

Transport

Trains
www.trenitalia.com

Buses
ATC
La Spezia to Porto Venere
tel 0187 522588
www.atcesercizio.it

Explora bus
La Spezia to Cinque Terre
www.explora5terre.it

Ferries
La Spezia–Porto Venere–Riomaggiore–
Manarola–Vernazza–Monterosso–
Levanto
www.navigazionegolfodeipoeti.it
tel 0187 732200.
These services operate from
April to October.

Porto Venere to Palmaria island
is year-round
tel 347 8024817
www.barcaioliportovenere.com.

APPENDIX D
Italian–English glossary

Italian	English
abbazia, badia	abbey
acqua (non) potabile	water (not) suitable for drinking
affittacamere	rooms for rent
agriturismo	farm stay
albergo	hotel
alimentari	groceries
alto	high
anello	ring, circuit
aperto	open
ascensore	lift
autostazione	bus station
basso	low
biglietto	ticket
biglietteria	ticket office
bivio	junction
bocca, valico	saddle, pass
borgo	village, town
bosco	wood
caccia	hunting
caduta roccia	rockfalls
cala, seno	bay, cove
canale, rio	stream
cappella	chapel
carruggio	narrow alley in Ligurian village
castello	castle
cava	quarry
chiesa	church
chiuso	closed

Italian	English
colla, colle	pass, saddle
collina	hill
croce	cross, crucifix
divieto di accesso	no entry
duomo	cathedral
enoteca	wine bar, shop
entrata	entrance
fermata bus	bus stop
ferrovia	railway
fiume	river
foce	mountain pass or river mouth
fontana, fonte, sorgente	fountain, spring
forte, fortezza	fortress, castle
fosso	gully, watercourse
frana	landslide
giardino	garden
grotta	cave
isola	island
locanda	guesthouse or restaurant
montagna, monte	mountain
mulino a vento	windmill
museo	museum
navetta	shuttle bus
ostello	hostel
osteria, trattoria	tavern, bar, restaurant
panificio	bakery

APPENDIX D – ITALIAN–ENGLISH GLOSSARY

Italian	English
percorso	route
pericolo, pericoloso	danger, dangerous
piazza	town square
podere	rural property
ponte	bridge
porta	door, gateway
pozzo	well
Pro Loco	local tourist office
proprietà privata	private property
rifugio	mountain refuge
santuario	church, sanctuary, hermitage
scoglio	offshore rock
sella	saddle
sentiero	path
sorgente	spring
spiaggia	beach
stazione ferroviaria	railway station
strada, via	road
strada bianca	unsealed country road
torre	tower
uscita	exit
vetta	summit
vietato	forbidden

Handy bus/train terminology

Italian	English
biglietto di andata (andata-ritorno)	single (return) ticket
cambio a ...	change at ...
coincidenza	connection

Italian	English
feriale	working days (Mon–Sat)
festivo	Sun and public hols
giornaliero	daily
sciopero	strike
scolastico	school term
soppresso	no service
da ... a ...	from ... to ... (dates)

Useful expressions

Italian	English
Do you speak English?	Parla inglese?
Good morning	Buongiorno
Good evening	Buona sera
Goodnight	Buona notte
Good-bye and thank you	Arrivederci e grazie
On the phone: Hello, I'd like a single/double room for tonight/tomorrow night	Pronto, vorrei una camera singola/ doppia per stasera/ domani sera
How much is it?	Quanto costa?
Can I pay with a credit card?	Posso pagare con la carta di credito?
Is breakfast included?	E' inclusa la colazione?
What time is breakfast/dinner?	A che ora è la colazione/cena?
I'm vegetarian/ vegan/celiac	Sono vegetariano/ vegano/celiaco
What's on today? (restaurant)	Che cosa c'è oggi?

APPENDIX E

Accommodation

Suggestions are given here for apartments, B&Bs and hotels convenient for walks.

Campiglia
Agriturismo Codemi
tel 349 6407889
www.codemincampiglia.com

Due Mari rooms
tel 335 5267797
naomo1973@gmail.com

Colla di Gritta
Albergo Monterosso Alto
tel 0187 801220
www.monterossoalto.eu

Corniglia
Ostello di Corniglia
tel 0187 812559
www.ostellocorniglia.com

Le Terrazze B&B
tel 349 8459684
www.eterasse.it

Levanto
Ostello Ospitalia del Mare
tel 0187 802562
http://ospitalialevanto.com

Case Lovara
www.poderecaselovara.it
(on the way to Punta Mesco)

Manarola
Ostello
tel 0187 920039
http://www.hostel5terre.it/it/
OstelloManarola

Alla Porta Rossa
tel 0187 920189
www.mareterra.it

Monte Muzzerone
(above Porto Venere)
Rifugio Muzzerone
tel 340 8098720
www.rifugiomuzzerone.it

Monterosso
Affittacamere Il Gabbiano
tel 0187 817578
www.affittacamereristorante-
ilgabbiano.com

Antica Terrazza
tel 347 1326213
www.anticaterrazza.com

Palmaria
Locanda Lorena
tel 0187 792370
www.locandalorena.com
open March to Oct

Portovenere
Ostello
tel 0187 792606

Hotel Genio
tel 0187 790611
www.hotelgenioportovenere.com

Prevo
Teresita Apartments
tel 348 7864808
www.teresitaapartments.yolasite.com

Riomaggiore
Hotel La Zorza
tel 0187 920036
www.hotelzorza.com

Alla Marina
tel 328 0134077
www.allamarina.com

Volastra
Il Vigneto B&B
tel 0187 1852727
www.ilvigneto5terre.com

Vernazza
Hotel Gianni Franzi
tel 0187 812228
www.giannifranzi.it

Albergo Barbara
tel 0187 812398
www.albergobarbara.it

Admiring the Ligurian Sea on Walk 12

Pozzale is on the southeast edge of the island of Palmaria (Walk 16)

DOWNLOAD THE ROUTES
IN GPX FORMAT

All the routes in this guide are available for download from:

www.cicerone.co.uk/973/GPX

as standard format GPX files. You should be able to load them into most online GPX systems and mobile devices, whether GPS or smartphone. You may need to convert the file into your preferred format using a conversion programme such as gpsvisualizer.com or one of the many other such websites and programmes.

When you follow this link, you will be asked for your email address and where you purchased the guidebook, and have the option to subscribe to the Cicerone e-newsletter.

www.cicerone.co.uk

LISTING OF CICERONE GUIDES

BRITISH ISLES CHALLENGES, COLLECTIONS AND ACTIVITIES
Cycling Land's End to John o' Groats
Great Walks on the England Coast Path
The Big Rounds
The Book of the Bivvy
The Book of the Bothy
The Mountains of England & Wales:
  Vol 1 Wales
  Vol 2 England
The National Trails
Walking the End to End Trail

SHORT WALKS SERIES
Short Walks Hadrian's Wall
Short Walks in Arnside and Silverdale
Short Walks in Nidderdale
Short Walks in the Lake District: Windermere Ambleside and Grasmere
Short Walks in the Surrey Hills
Short Walks on the Malvern Hills

SCOTLAND
Ben Nevis and Glen Coe
Cycle Touring in Northern Scotland
Cycling in the Hebrides
Great Mountain Days in Scotland
Mountain Biking in Southern and Central Scotland
Mountain Biking in West and North West Scotland
Not the West Highland Way Scotland
Scotland's Mountain Ridges
Scottish Wild Country Backpacking
Skye's Cuillin Ridge Traverse
The Borders Abbeys Way
The Great Glen Way
The Great Glen Way Map Booklet
The Hebridean Way
The Hebrides
The Isle of Mull
The Isle of Skye
The Skye Trail
The Southern Upland Way
The Speyside Way Map Booklet
The West Highland Way
The West Highland Way Map Booklet
Walking Ben Lawers, Rannoch and Atholl
Walking in the Cairngorms
Walking in the Pentland Hills
Walking in the Scottish Borders
Walking in the Southern Uplands
Walking in Torridon, Fisherfield, Fannichs and An Teallach
Walking Loch Lomond and the Trossachs
Walking on Arran
Walking on Harris and Lewis
Walking on Jura, Islay and Colonsay
Walking on Rum and the Small Isles
Walking on the Orkney and Shetland Isles
Walking on Uist and Barra
Walking the Cape Wrath Trail
Walking the Corbetts:
  Vol 1 South of the Great Glen
  Vol 2 North of the Great Glen
Walking the Galloway Hills
Walking the John o' Groats Trail
Walking the Munros
  Vol 1 – Southern, Central and Western Highlands
  Vol 2 – Northern Highlands and the Cairngorms
Winter Climbs: Ben Nevis and Glen Coe

NORTHERN ENGLAND ROUTES
Cycling the Reivers Route
Cycling the Way of the Roses
Hadrian's Cycleway
Hadrian's Wall Path
Hadrian's Wall Path Map Booklet
The C2C Cycle Route
The Coast to Coast Cycle Route
The Coast to Coast Walk
The Coast to Coast Walk Map Booklet
The Pennine Way
The Pennine Way Map Booklet
Walking the Dales Way
Walking the Dales Way Map Booklet

NORTH-EAST ENGLAND, YORKSHIRE DALES AND PENNINES
Cycling in the Yorkshire Dales
Great Mountain Days in the Pennines
Mountain Biking in the Yorkshire Dales
St Oswald's Way and St Cuthbert's Way
The Cleveland Way and the Yorkshire Wolds Way
The Cleveland Way Map Booklet
The North York Moors
The Reivers Way
Trail and Fell Running in the Yorkshire Dales
Walking in County Durham
Walking in Northumberland
Walking in the North Pennines
Walking in the Yorkshire Dales: North and East
Walking in the Yorkshire Dales: South and West

NORTH-WEST ENGLAND AND THE ISLE OF MAN
Cycling the Pennine Bridleway
Isle of Man Coastal Path
The Lancashire Cycleway
The Lune Valley and Howgills
Walking in Cumbria's Eden Valley
Walking in Lancashire
Walking in the Forest of Bowland and Pendle
Walking on the Isle of Man
Walking on the West Pennine Moors
Walks in Silverdale and Arnside

LAKE DISTRICT
Bikepacking in the Lake District
Cycling in the Lake District
Great Mountain Days in the Lake District
Joss Naylor's Lakes, Meres and Waters of the Lake District
Lake District Winter Climbs
Lake District: High Level and Fell Walks
Lake District: Low Level and Lake Walks
Mountain Biking in the Lake District
Outdoor Adventures with Children – Lake District
Scrambles in the Lake District – North
Scrambles in the Lake District – South
Trail and Fell Running in the Lake District
Walking The Cumbria Way
Walking the Lake District Fells –
  Borrowdale
  Buttermere
  Coniston
  Keswick
  Langdale
  Mardale and the Far East
  Patterdale
  Wasdale
Walking the Tour of the Lake District

DERBYSHIRE, PEAK DISTRICT AND MIDLANDS
Cycling in the Peak District
Dark Peak Walks
Scrambles in the Dark Peak
Walking in Derbyshire
Walking in the Peak District – White Peak East
Walking in the Peak District – White Peak West

CICERONE

Trust Cicerone to guide your next adventure,
wherever it may be around the world...

Discover guides for hiking, mountain walking, backpacking,
trekking, trail running, cycling and mountain biking, ski touring,
climbing and scrambling in Britain, Europe and worldwide.

Connect with Cicerone online and find inspiration.

- buy books and ebooks
- articles, advice and trip reports
- podcasts and live events
- GPX files and updates
- regular newsletter

cicerone.co.uk